Stolen Lives

Stolen Lives
Trading women into sex and slavery

Sietske Altink

Scarlet Press • London

Harrington Park Press • New York

An Imprint of Haworth Press, Inc.

Published in 1995 by Scarlet Press
5 Montague Road, London E8 2HN

Published by Harrington Park Press
(an imprint of Haworth Press, Inc.)
in the United States for
North and South America
ISBN: 1–56023–885–2
Library of Congress Catalog Card Number 95–80629

First published in 1993 under the title
Dossier Vrouwenhandel by Uitgeverij Sua, Amsterdam

British Library Cataloguing-in-Publication Data
A catalogue record for this book is available from
the British Library

ISBN   1 85727 097 5 pb
ISBN   1 85727 003 7 hb

Designed and produced for Scarlet Press by
Chase Production Services, Chipping Norton
Typeset from author's disk by
Stanford DTP Services, Milton Keynes
Printed in the EC by J. W. Arrowsmith

Contents

For the woman who called herself Victoria

Preface

'Shocking': this is the reaction when traffic in women receives publicity. But wherever we live – in Europe, the United States or Asia – the problem exists, and it cannot be attributed to the naïveté of its victims, as the cases recorded in this book show.

In my work for the Dutch foundation against traffic in women, Stichting Tegen Vrouwenhandel (STV) and my research among prostitutes, I have studied a number of cases of trafficking. I have talked to more than 100 women suspected of entering the Netherlands through the channels of the traffic. For this book, which was first published in Dutch, I interviewed 20: three Thai women, three Colombians, five women from the Dominican Republic, one Moroccan, one Indonesian, plus a woman from Poland and another from former Yugoslavia. One wanted to say only that she was of Asian origin. The remaining women came from the Philippines. The group is a fair representation of the nationalities of Third World women trafficked to Europe. Some of the cases show how the trade in people can be adapted to local conditions.

As the traffickers are highly organized, most of their victims dare not speak out. Ana from the Dominican Republic said, 'They were like a mafia. I couldn't even discuss my situation with other girls. Whenever I told someone my story, the next day the traffickers knew that I had talked. The man who kept me prisoner explicitly forbade me to speak to other girls. If these criminals have the address of your parents' home, they can keep you a prisoner. They say you endanger your father and mother when you don't obey them. That's how the traffickers subdue us.' Because of their reluctance to talk, it made no sense to search brothels or red light districts for trafficked women. Indeed, when I did this, I would end up talking to the owners of the brothels and not the women.

By the time I interviewed them, most of the women I talked to were safe and the traffickers had no further hold over them. They had run away or were in contact with the police. However, a few of them were still being pressured by profiteers offering them dubious forms of help, usually for considerable sums of money.

One essential problem that most trafficked women face is that they are seen by the authorities as illegal immigrants rather than as refugees and it is therefore difficult for them to give evidence against their traffickers. Most of the women I talked to were not keen to relive their painful experiences. Celestina of the Dominican Republic said, 'I only tell my story to warn other girls. I don't really want to talk. When I tell you what happened in that particular period in my life, I forget to look after my daughter and I can only think of what that criminal organization did to me. That is not right. I should be thinking of my child's future.'

In the confined world which these women inhabit rumour is an important source of information. All the women I came across knew of cases of trafficking other than their own. One Dominican woman called this communication system of the powerless the 'Arabian telephone'. I have checked and double-checked these rumours as far as possible and asked people in their vicinity for background information. Not all the rumours are reliable, however. Sometimes the traffickers spread stories whose sole purpose is to disinform the women. For example, some women trafficked by the so-called Billionaire gang were told that one gang member had cut a victim in pieces and put her in the freezer, which is in fact the plot of a well-known Roald Dahl story.

The Netherlands have been the starting point for my research, but the methods used by traffickers to the Netherlands apply to most other countries, and the cases I have reconstructed illustrate the methods of recruitment used by traffickers and the problems the women they traffic encounter elsewhere. Research in Germany and Belgium has shown that the fight against traffic in women in those countries faces the same problems as in the Netherlands: women who dare not speak out and the difficulty of finding proof. Personal histories which have been published in these countries have much in common with the stories of women in the Netherlands.

It is virtually impossible to compile a complete picture of traffic in women in every corner of the world. Apart from Asia and some western European countries, statistics are hard to come by. Most data on traffic is gathered by non-governmental organizations and women's groups. Apart from the interviews, my own data comes from brochures and publications by women's groups which fight trafficking. Newspapers and television were also important sources of information, the newspaper reports being translations of stories from international press agencies which appeared in Dutch newspapers. The vast body of documentation at STV and court cases in the Netherlands were also important sources.

This is not an encyclopaedic or scientific survey: it is rather a journalistic exploration with its own limitations of time and space. The cases of traffic in women for prostitution which I describe range from the small to the large scale. Women are usually forced into small-scale trafficking by one or two people; their husbands, for instance. In large-scale traffic a network run by international organized crime wholesales in people and makes use of contacts in high places. Chapter 1 defines what I believe trafficking to be and some of its characteristics. After looking at its history and international context in chapters 2 and 3, I consider the Dutch scene in chapter 4. Chapters 5 to 11 are more specific and are based on my interviews. They reconstruct traffickers' methods and routes from specific cases. They also contain some international information, for instance on South America, which is not included in chapter 3. Chapters 12 and 13 consider the plight of mail-order brides and domestic workers. In conclusion, Chapter 14 looks at measures that could be taken to prevent trafficking and there is also a list of contact addresses for organizations mentioned in the book.

To preserve their anonymity, the names of the interviewees have been altered, as have personal details such as the number of children they have. Traffickers' names have also been changed in some instances.

Acknowledgments

My work with STV has been all important in writing this book. I want to thank all my colleagues there for their stimulating conversation, their friendship and for the expertise they shared with me.

I am also grateful to the following organizations and people, who are listed in alphabetical order – by first name, where relevant, as some people cannot be mentioned by their full names: AGISRA, Germany (Arbeitsgemeinschaft Gegen Internationale Sexuelle und Rassistische Ausbeutung); Al Dunnette; Amsterdam Call Girls, for additional information on Dutch prostitution; anonymous – most of all I am indebted to the trafficked women and non-trafficked migrant prostitutes who dared to share their experiences with me; the Anti-Slavery Society, London branch; the Asian Women's Resource Centre, London; Avis Lewallen, who had her house overrun by a panicky author from the Netherlands while the book was being edited; Bayanihan, the foundation for the well-being of Filipinos in the Netherlands; the BBC for involving me in the *Inside Story* documentary 'The Women Trade'; Belgrade's hotline for women – Violetta Krasnic and Zorica Mrsevic; Ben Stam, my husband, for his priceless practical support; Brid Brennan, who works for the Transnational Institute in Amsterdam; CFMW, the Commission of Filipino Migrant Workers; the Chinese Community Centre in Gerrard Street, London; Chris de Stoop for sharing information with me; churches – I would like to thank the following churches for their financial support while I was writing the Dutch edition of the book: Projectencommissie van de Dominicanessen, Provincialaat Kruisheren and the Zending en Werelddiakonaat van de Gereformeerde Kerken in the Netherlands; CRI, the Criminal Intelligence Unit, Interpol, the Netherlands, especially Leen Pieterse; the English Collective of Prostitutes (ECP); Fe Jusay for introductions in London; FIZ, the Frauen Information Zentrum, Mechteld Mauer; Heinrich Böll Institute, for taking me to Prague to meet organizations and experts involved in trafficking; Hester van Vugt, for advice on the Dutch edition;

Humanitas, Social Welfare for Prostitutes, Door Malkus; Hydra ('Next whisky bar'); Ine Ploumen at the working group on traffic in women in Limburg; Jean Gould of Winstanley Burgess, London; Kalayaan, the organization for support to migrant workers in London – without Aye, Lourdes, Margaret, Maria and Speedy the section on domestic slavery could not have been written; Liz Cowen, for her hospitality for ten days, and for managing to do an excellent job of editing the book; Lourdes – unfortunately I can't list her family name, she let me stay in her hide-out while I was doing research in London and taught me some of the dry humour that goes with being an 'unauthorized domestic worker'; Mama Cash, an organization which invests in women's projects in the Netherlands, which helped to produce the Dutch edition; Maria Koers, advocate general in the Netherlands, for legal advice for the Dutch edition; Meester A. de Graafstichting, Institute for Prostitution Affairs, Amsterdam, for the free use of the archives and for information; MVP, working group, Men, Women and Prostitution, the organization of clients of prostitutes in the Netherlands; Payoke (and Saralek) for letting me stay with them for a couple of days; the Philippine embassy in the Netherlands; the police departments of Limburg-Noord and Rotterdam; Priscilla Alexander of the National Task Force on Prostitution in the United States; Rode Draad, the organization of Dutch prostitutes; Rohlee de Guzman; Verenjin Exploitanten Relaxhuizen (VER), the Dutch organization for owners of relaxhouses.

1 The characteristics of traffic

'My brother had warned me against traffickers in women. I never imagined that I myself was going to have to deal with them. I had heard about women who were sold to Japan, but I didn't realize it also happened in Europe.' Before Fatima, who comes from Indonesia, became a victim of the traffic in women and found herself in the Netherlands she had considered trafficking to be a marginal phenomenon, as most people do.

The idea of trafficking in women is associated in many people's minds with the 'white slave trade', with European girls being kidnapped and taken to harems in the Middle East. In the 1960s and 1970s the stories were numerous. Paris and Brussels were considered dangerous places for young girls: they would be lured into expensive shops, from where they would be whisked through a trapdoor in the floor into the cellars and never seen again. Or an elderly woman would ask girls to help her up the stairs, only to lock them up. Not unnaturally these reports were treated with scepticism. It comes as a shock therefore to realize that traffic in women for prostitution by professional criminal gangs is happening here and now.

Women are trafficked not only to Europe but worldwide, not only from south to north, but from Latin America to southern Europe and the Middle East, from south-east Asia to the Middle East and central and northern Europe, from South America to North America and Europe, and from eastern Europe to western Europe. To traffic women means to work upon their desire or need to migrate, by bringing them into prostitution under conditions that make them totally dependent on their recruiters in ways which also impair their rights. It exists where poverty has forced women to seek different methods of survival for themselves and their families. And it takes different forms for the women involved, not only prostitution but also domestic slavery or mail-order marriage.

According to United Nations official Jean Fernand-Laurent, trafficking in women is more profitable than arms or drug smuggling.

The concept of victim is the only one available to describe trafficked women. The word is used here in the legal sense: when you are robbed you are the victim of a crime. However, 'victim' has unwanted connotations of meekness and submissiveness which echo Victorian demands that victims of trafficking should be chaste and ignorant, a definition that ignores the sense of responsibility which leads women to migrate in search of work. Many women from the Third and Second Worlds realize their goal of maintaining their families with money earned in the First World. Yet women who don't seem submissive and innocent are still not taken seriously.

Women who dare to expose their traffickers encounter a barrage of questions in which the onus is on them to prove that they are victims. A former Dutch attorney, who is now an advocate general, Maria Koers, has often handled cases of trafficking. 'If a girl has a well-oiled tongue, it is very difficult to convince the judges that she was exploited. But a woman who speaks up can also fall victim to traffickers. The lawyer for the defence might say, "If that girl had so much initiative, she could easily have avoided her plight." But then they don't realize that the woman had virtually no choice.'

'It hurts, but don't call me a poor thing,' one woman I interviewed said. Victims can also be very tough who will do anything to avenge the damage done to them and make a better life for themselves. Some victims don't go to the police but start trafficking themselves, or side with the traffickers to avoid reprisals. After all, they know the ins and outs of the trade and so think they have less to fear. They believe they can make a new career as a trafficker.

The recent wave of trafficking has been driven by poverty in the Third World, which forces women to migrate from rural areas to the cities in search of better economic opportunities. Many of them then become part of the sex-tourism trade, which bolsters the balance of payments in their own country, or they migrate to the richer countries of the First World. A similar lack of opportunity and employment in eastern European countries and the new ease of movement between east and west have drawn women into western Europe.

Estimates of the numbers of women who are victims of trafficking vary considerably because they depend on the definition of what trafficking is. If every migrant sex worker is considered a victim of the traffic in people, then large numbers can be splashed across newspaper headlines. Thousands or even millions of women are supposed to be trafficked worldwide, depending on the newspaper you read.[1] If the numbers are exaggerated in this way then the problem becomes so enormous that it is impossible to tackle. Nor are the victims helped if the problem is played down. Because of the nature of trafficking, it is difficult for women to come forward and say they have been trafficked, and therefore difficult to estimate how many women are its victims. Moreover, most foreign prostitutes in Europe are not victims of trafficking but are illegal immigrants, and they also won't speak out. Many prostitutes migrate voluntarily, by so-called chain migration: friends, sisters or nieces invite them over.[2] Most migrant prostitutes arrive on tourist visas which don't allow them to work, in prostitution or any other profession. And not all sex workers from outside the European Union are illegal immigrants. Some have permits of residence, through marriage for example.

What is trafficking?

Not all prostitutes are victims of traffic in women or sex slaves, as they are sometimes called. At first sight trafficking might seem to have many similarities with the slave trade. Like trafficked women, slaves had to work long hours and were punished when they didn't work hard enough. However, the main difference between the two lies in the nature of the labour performed. Slaves did 'normal', recognized labour. Prostitutes don't. Domestic labour is a borderline case: it can be undertaken with proper rights and pay, but it can also be informal, unpaid labour.

In European law legislators have carefully avoided equating the trade in women with slavery because they were afraid they would implicitly recognize prostitution as labour if they did so. At the start of the twentieth century traffic in women was considered to be immoral rather than exploitative. The emphasis was placed on the moral deterioration of the women. By stigmatizing the female victims of traffic as prostitutes who don't perform labour, the women were marginalized. The official view was that women who were trafficked could not be called slaves in case prostitution was thereby recognized as labour.[3]

A characteristic of the slave trade is the direct buying and selling of people; this also occurs in some cases of trafficking. Clients with whom the women get involved have to buy their release. One punter had to buy a second victim at half price. In one criminal case the suspects were charged with the offence of slave trading, but the case was dismissed.

The idea that traffic in women is a matter of sexual violence has also been abandoned, although forced prostitution is still considered to be sexual violence because women don't have sexual autonomy. However, even when women don't object to working as prostitutes they may be victims of economic exploitation. Sexual violence may be involved because some women have been raped or forced to work without a condom.

Since violation of physical or sexual autonomy is involved, traffic in women is also a human rights issue. It violates articles 4, 5 and 13 of the Universal Declaration of Human Rights. Trafficked women don't have freedom of movement or freedom of speech and in some cases are forced to migrate, for example when they are abducted.

Transporting women is a reflection of the role migration and organized crime play in trafficking. Most modern traffickers have developed their criminal activities from current major political issues: the tension between the desire of the Third and Second World peoples to migrate to the First World and the restrictions western countries place on immigration. Traffickers exploit the political void at the heart of migration issues.

The crime of trafficking arises from political expediency.[4] Criminals take advantage of the fact that politicians don't deal effectively with controversial problems. This political dimension is absent in 'ordinary' serious crime. Criminality arising out of political expediency presupposes a flexibility that is only feasible in organized groups. Traffickers need to make contacts with the legitimate world. They do so, for instance, by replacing a failing administration in the women's home countries with their own systems for forging documents. Trafficking women is labour intensive. The women have to be brought to the target country, distributed, watched over and housed by the traffickers, who can't operate without contacts in the women's home countries. The gangs use other methods characteristic of organized crime: they work with corrupt authorities, launder money, have contacts in both legitimate areas and the underworld and form a hierarchy in which there is a division of labour. Only small-scale trafficking, for instance trafficking for marriage, cannot be described as organized crime. Among their other activities, most organized crime groups – the Italian and Russian mafia, the Japanese yakuza and Chinese triads – all traffic in women.

Recruiting with a false promise of marriage is the oldest trick in the book. Another classic trick is to promise a job through personal contacts. Other methods include abduction, or promises of a holiday, a student grant, political asylum or a visa based on a phoney job offer from a company. Leen Pieterse of the Criminal Intelligence Unit in the Netherlands said, 'We are alerted when one company invites a few hundred Russian girls to work with them as secretaries.' Brazilian and eastern European women especially are led to believe they can combine a holiday with a job. Large-scale recruitment is done by agencies which promise women jobs or a career as an entertainer. Some women really believe they are going to be trained as ballet dancers. In one case the traffickers followed an eastern European ballet company which was touring Europe, went to the performances and kidnapped one of the most beautiful dancers.

The number of abductions is increasing. Before 1991 there were none, but since then six cases were recorded in 1994.[5] Leen Pieterse said, 'Sometimes these girls are offered drinks laced with drugs and they are then raped in a hotel room. Pictures are taken to blackmail them with afterwards. Maybe these men don't intend initially to force the woman into prostitution, but she has to be disposed of and they daren't kill her. The easiest way out is to make her disappear into the underworld of prostitution. It is also possible that a girl has slept with a guy and he has paid for her drinks; she felt sorry afterwards and didn't dare to go back home to her parents.'

All nationalities, black and white, men and women, Bosnians and Serbs, eastern and western Europeans, work together to traffic women. Traffickers are all ages and come from all professions. Some are better educated than the police – one suspect, for example, had graduated in theology – others are virtually illiterate. He or she may be a player in a national football team (which has happened), a grandmother, a small-time criminal or a well-dressed manager. It is difficult to talk to suspected traffickers because the nature of their profession makes them hard to track down. The one person suspected of trafficking whom I managed to interview talked a lot without saying much.

The women they have trafficked could provide first-hand information about them. The victims of small-scale gangs in particular could give the details of their daily, usually violent, contact with the traffickers. In general the women who have escaped from large-scale traffickers had little to do with the big bosses, but had more contact with their staff. However, something about the motives of the traffickers, their frame of mind and their personalities can be gleaned from trials where they have had to defend themselves, though it should be remembered that in the court room they are in a strange environment.

One sex-club owner who was accused of trafficking women wouldn't even admit that he was involved in the sex industry. He said that he provided a social service. The judge was not convinced. Some other traffickers presented their activities as development aid, saying they only wanted to help the women. The excuses traffickers find are usually very lame: one Yugoslavian suspect said at his trial that the women were conspiring against him because they wanted another pimp. Another could not believe that he had done anything wrong. 'Why do my girls always go to the police?' he asked. He was convicted.

Thousands of documented cases of traffic in women in Europe now exist. Since 1992, however, there has been an increase in the traffic of eastern and central European women in the Netherlands. For example, in 1993, 75 per cent of STV's clients came from eastern European countries, which increased to 80 per cent in 1994. For the English edition of this book, which has been revised and extended, I talked to some of these eastern European women. Through STV's contacts abroad I was also able to speak to some victims and informants in Belgium and Britain. Most of the women interviewed in the Netherlands were clients of STV. Kalayaan (Freedom), an organization of migrant Philippine women, also introduced me to women who were traded as mail-order brides and domestic workers.

In Germany the traffic in mail-order brides and domestic workers is well established; in the Netherlands and other European countries, however, it is a relatively new phenomenon. Because household labour is not formalized, organizations have been able to abuse women's rights and trade in them as domestic helpers. Mail-order brides are expected to work as unpaid domestic helpers and to deliver sexual services for free. Both these areas are defined as trafficking in women because they exploit women in the areas in which they work traditionally but which are not recognized, let alone formalized, as labour.

Although the trafficking in males and children is outside the scope of this book, it should not be thought that it is only women who are trafficked. Recently a ring trafficking Czech boys was discovered. Brazilian transvestites are also trafficked. Trafficked men have the same rights in the Netherlands as female victims, but as yet there are no shelters for them. A social worker in Rotterdam, Door Malkus, who works with male as well as female prostitutes, said to me, 'Traffic in boys may occur in large numbers. And in children too for that matter.' However, most traffic in children takes place for the illegal adoption market. Occasionally the papers report traffic in boys from eastern European orphanages, usually for paedophiles or for men and women who hope that sex with minors will decrease the risk of contracting AIDS. There is also a market for child pornography, which people who are so minded can easily make in their own homes with camcorders. Millions of children are supposed to be abused worldwide. Unfortunately stories of child trafficking are usually sensationalized. Reports of satanic child abuse, that is to say unverified accounts of children being abused by rings of satanists in isolated houses in the countryside, do much harm. They distract public attention from the many real victims of child trafficking.[6]

2 Traffic old and new

Trafficking in women is not new, but has been practised for thousands of years. In some instances it has been sanctioned by religious custom, in others it has been the result of war or great industrial changes. Traditionally women have been treated as a commodity to be bartered or sold. For example, in the sixth century the Roman Emperor Justinian (527–65) wrote:

> We have learnt that many of our subjects, finding that the profits they get from prostitutes are insufficient, are travelling throughout Europe and by taking advantage of poverty and inexperienced young girls, seduce them with promises of fine clothes and other things of a like nature. That they keep them in their houses by means of a contract which they make them sign, stipulating that they shall stay in a brothel as long as the brothelkeeper shall judge fit.[1]

Justinian detailed practices by traffickers which are still used: debt bondage, confiscation of earnings and the denial of sleep and food. However, the phenomenon he described was not categorized as traffic in women until the nineteenth century.

The nineteenth century

In the nineteenth century heartrending stories circulated in various European countries about young girls who were being abused for prostitution. They were recruited with false promises of jobs abroad, but once they had reached the brothels they could only leave when they had paid the debts they were supposed to have incurred for clothing, food and lodging.

The stories concerned girls from France, Belgium and Germany who were trafficked to licensed state brothels in various European countries. Balkestein, who investigated the subject in the nineteenth century in both target and receiving countries, looked at these claims.[2] He came across several cases, for instance that of Félicie Dordoigne, who was born in 1882, and at 18 years of age was a minor under the law of the time. She told him:

> I am one of the many daughters of a poor widow. I went to Paris to find a job. While I was looking at advertisements on a newsstand in Paris, two gentlemen approached me. They asked me whether I was looking for employment. I answered I wanted to work as a seamstress. The men suggested they had suitable employment in a large house in the Netherlands.

When she told them she was 18 and could not travel without her parents' permission, they provided her with a forged birth certificate. She was then introduced to a third man, who turned out to be a brothel-owner. He took her to the station, where he handed her a letter for her future employer. She was told to take a horse and carriage when she reached Amsterdam. When she finally arrived at her destination, the truth dawned on her. She was in a brothel. As soon as she could, she escaped with the help of her colleagues, but she had no time to put on her shoes and was found barefoot outside the brothel.

Whereas German and French girls in the Netherlands ended up in closed houses, Belgian women had to sit behind windows 'in drawing-room costumes, behind semi-transparent curtains'.

The trafficker's progress

At the beginning of the twentieth century there was a large traffic of women between Britain and the United States. It was estimated that American brothels employed about 300,000 prostitutes. As each one worked on average in prostitution for five years, some 60,000 had to be replaced annually.[3] Some women were recruited in shops by men posing as customers. 'He delivered me from the slavery in the shop. But I was so stupid as to believe him,' one shop assistant stated in court.

A famous American procurer of women was Paul Sinclair, born in 1875 in Ohio, who later repented and became active in the fight against traffic in women. He later confessed, 'I lived a life of lust, greed and avarice.' He used the classic tricks of the trafficker: debts and threats. At the end of his career he made it up with one of his victims and remained her friend for life. His contemporaries believed that trafficking arose from ignorance, double standards, immoral literature, theatre entertainment and dance halls. Parents who failed to supervise their daughters or who didn't caution their sons to avoid brothels were blamed and fathers who frequented brothels were reminded that prostitutes had fathers too. Pressure groups achieved the closure of brothels. And after the United States introduced strict immigration laws in 1924 it became increasingly difficult to import foreign prostitutes. Traffickers consequently had to resort to bogus marriages to get foreign women into the country. Prostitution did not disappear in the United States but became an illegal activity organized by criminals. Thanks to the illegal liquor trade during Prohibition, the mafia became well organized. It moved on into drugs and prostitution when Prohibition was lifted.

Salvatore 'Lucky' Luciano was the first mafioso to engage in traffic in women. Some 10,000 girls were supposed to have worked in brothels controlled by his mob. About 100 women who refused to co-operate were beaten to death. Finally a woman blew the whistle on him and he was sentenced to 30 years in prison.[4]

Kaftans

The centres of nineteenth-century intercontinental traffic were the Jewish ghettoes in eastern Europe.[5] Jewish trafficking in women was the sad result of anti-semitism, urbanization, secularization and the demand for prostitutes. Eastern Europe was overpopulated and impoverished. In the ghettoes several families would share a single room, their spaces only marked out by a chalk line. Around 1910 there was a huge shortage of potential husbands, and unmarried daughters were considered a burden on their impoverished families. However, they could only leave the community with the 'yellow badge of shame', which showed that they were prostitutes. Because there were no brothels in the ghetto, they had to go elsewhere and a number of women gratefully accepted this passport as an opportunity to see the world.

Other 'fallen' women were rejected by their fathers. Many eligible women were married according to the Jewish ritual of Stillah Chuppah, a ceremony which didn't have civil status although a rabbi was present. These women were then completely dependent on their husbands, who could easily blackmail them into prostitution.

The *kaftan* or marriage broker was a familiar institution in Jewish communities. Though *kaftans* were not originally traffickers, the two words later became synonymous. They rounded up girls in Russian Poland and Galicia to send to brothels. Galicia was part of the Austro-Hungarian empire, bordering on Russia. Its centre was Lemberg. Most of the brothels in the region were owned by Jews, who were allowed to run them unhindered by the police. Although brothels were more or less accepted, the Jewish community ostracized the unclean people who were their victims.

As industrial centres, mining areas and construction sites in South America and elsewhere expanded rapidly in the 1880s, there was massive migration from Galicia. The large concentrations of labourers in these areas meant there was a great demand for prostitutes. *Kaftans* soon began trafficking women to South America and Constantinople and even to the Far East. Women who started in brothels in their local neighbourhood ended up in Argentina, for instance, which had a large Jewish community. The pioneer of the traffic, David Auerbach, was invited by the Jesuits, no less, to remedy the shortage of women in Buenos Aires. Pimps had arrived in Argentina before the first influx of eastern Europeans.

In 1898 the Jewish Colonization Association worked on 28 cases of trafficking. Only three of the girls were not Jewish. However, the records are not completely reliable because they don't always distinguish between traffickers, victims and independent prostitutes. Women already on the game were only too glad to get away from bad working conditions in eastern Europe and become high-class prostitutes in Argentina. This ambition was thwarted by the control the traffickers had over them. The girls could not migrate on their own because it was reputed to be very dangerous for women to travel alone. Some villain would see to it that when a woman had to change trains, she would miss the connection.[6] The recruitment methods were similar to those used today: false promises of jobs, marriage and riches. For example, a man called Hirschfeld sold cheap rings at the doors of poor Jewish families in Pest, claiming he could introduce his victims to rich Turkish businessmen.

Usually trafficking was a family affair. The widow Chave Blum was the head of her family. When she was interrogated by the police at the respectable age of 86 she had established her offspring comfortably in the trade. One of her sons, a pimp, married a prostitute and was deported to Constantinople. Her other son owned a brothel in Buenos Aires. Her daughter had disappeared to Argentina after marrying a thief. In trafficking families the men were active as well as the women.

In 1892 in Lemberg 27 people were tried for trafficking 29 women, almost as if every woman had been taken care of personally. In those days traffickers could not bundle large groups of women on to planes and check on them long distance by telephone. But traffickers were quick to make use of any new technical developments. In Poland between 1875 and 1880 the railways were being built and shipping routes mapped out, both of which greatly helped traffickers. In one case women were lured on to a boat which sailed suddenly without warning, too late for the women to disembark.

The Zwi Migdal society in Argentina, called after its legendary founder, was the largest and most organized example of Jewish trafficking. Originally founded to run a cemetery for 'unclean persons' who were not allowed room in official burial grounds, it performed other social services for its members and soon became a cover for criminal activities like trafficking. Zwi Migdal was large and well connected and reputedly trafficked scores of women.

A Romanian called Derderian followed in the footsteps of Zwi Migdal. Working with Polish, Romanian and Bulgarian agents, he recruited his women through advertisements and had a special department which forged the necessary papers. Sometimes he would even send a secretary to the woman's home to make a trustworthy impression on her parents.[7]

In the twentieth century Jewish traffickers were dispersed all over the world. Eastern European traffickers directed their attention to North America, which they had avoided at first. French pimps had been the first to supply this market. Known as *maquereaux*, these pimps even had a costume to show who they were: velvet trousers, a blouse and a little silk cap. They were soon joined by pimps from Greece, Italy and the United States.[8] In Austria, where anti-semitism was very strong, right-wing groups used the part played by Jews in trafficking women for propagandist purposes. Anti-semites did not mention the large part other Jewish organizations played in combating the trafficking, and their other efforts to make amends for the crimes of the *kaftans*. In some cases their representatives waited at railway stations to catch traffickers in the act.

Abolitionism

In western Europe the fight against traffic in women was more systematic than in eastern Europe. In countries like the United Kingdom trafficking was to become a moral issue, which had a great impact on the later debate. The discussion was initiated by Josephine Butler (1828–1906), one of the first British activists against trafficking. Butler held the state responsible for the exploitation of women in brothels. She was convinced that the state condoned forced prostitution and exploitation of women and opposed the current view that prostitutes were necessary to satisfy the biological needs of men, who would otherwise harass respectable women, an opinion which she believed was the main cause of trafficking.

Many men and women joined Butler's movement. The men, however, tended to ignore the fact that she fought not only trafficking but also the belief that men could not control themselves. They preferred to concentrate on visiting brothels to rescue girls. Butler resented this. She wrote:

> Some men who worked with us at the beginning, shocked with the cruelty and illegality of the acts, fall off when they understand the thoroughness of our crusade, and that it is directed not only against the cruel result of vice, but against the tacit permission, the indisputable right as some have learned to regard it, granted to men to be impure at all.[9]

W.T. Stead, who edited the *Pall Mall Gazette*, became involved in the movement after hearing reports of abuse and torture in London brothels. Politicians and the judiciary were unmoved by the evidence, so Stead and Butler decided on a plan which would prove conclusively that virgins, some of them very young, were being trafficked. He would find a procurer, who would buy a child and take her through all the stages of trafficking short of sexual abuse. A reformed procuress, Rebecca Jarrett, who was also a member of the movement, found Eliza Armstrong, who was only 13. Stead gave Jarrett £5 to buy Eliza, and told her to make sure that Eliza's parents knew she was being bought for immoral purposes. Eliza's mother was arrested the same night for being drunk and disorderly on the proceeds of the sale. Without Butler's knowledge, Stead and Jarrett had Eliza's virginity tested by a midwife who was used by brothels to certify that young girls were virgins. Butler was furious when she heard of the means Stead had used to prove his case, but he had his story. When he published it in the *Pall Mall Gazette*, public rioting ensued and the paper was temporarily banned. Infuriated by this curb on the freedom of the press, George Bernard Shaw went out on the streets himself to sell the paper.

Butler left alone those women who had chosen to become prostitutes and had not been forced on to the game, but many of her followers condemned all prostitution. Well-meaning ladies founded organizations to 'lift the spirits' of prostitutes. Traffic in women was considered a moral issue by these groups, who ignored the social and economic bases of the problem.[10]

By the start of the twentieth century the idea that all prostitution, voluntary and involuntary, is slavery, had become dominant in Europe and the United States. The protagonists of this idea did not see prostitution as paid labour, but as the permanent subjection of women. They believed that prostitution should be abolished, as slavery had been, and called themselves abolitionists after those who had striven to abolish slavery. To distinguish traffic in women from the trade in negro slaves, the controversial term 'white slaves' was coined, which was later to be associated with forced prostitution. They wanted to force governments to ban both forced and voluntary prostitution.[11]

Another group, which wanted to end all state interference in prostitution, confusingly also called itself abolitionist. There were, therefore, three types of abolitionist organization: one which fought black slavery; a second, which wanted to ban all prostitution; and the third, which aimed to end state interference in prostitution. Josephine Butler belonged to the third group, but soon had to give in to dissenting opinions.

In 1902 there was an important conference on the abolition of traffic in women in Paris. Delegates agreed that by definition white slaves must be unmarried. This was to become enshrined in law in Massachusetts in the same year:

> the procuring must be fraudulent and deceitful and the woman must be unmarried and of a chaste life. If the procurer married the girl to circumvent the law, he cannot be prosecuted. If the girl makes one mistake in life, she cannot be protected from being procured.

The issue of the victims' virtue was to have long-term consequences. Until the 1980s only women of unblemished reputation could be labelled victims of traffic. Further, the delegates to the conference established that only international transport of women could be regarded as traffic in women, a view which still informs current discussion.

By the 1900s the feminist zeal had gone out of the movement as it became associated with moral reform. Contemporary feminists like Christabel Pankhurst and Emma Goldman considered the moral stand on prostitution fruitless. They wanted to improve women's economic position, so eradicating prostitution, and gave priority to the fight for the vote for women. Teresa Billington-Grieg from the Pankhursts' Women's Social and Political Union was even more cynical: 'There is no organised trapping, there is only sensationalism.'[12]

Trafficking in women had increased greatly with the first wave of industrialization in the nineteenth century. Large groups of people were dislocated as men moved into towns and cities to find employment, leaving women behind in the countryside. Middle-class indignation about prostitution and trafficking was increased by fears about urbanization. Cities like London were transformed and class divisions were challenged by workers demonstrating for their rights in rich neighbourhoods. Jack the Ripper then appeared on the scene, murdering women who went out to work.[13] The cities seemed to be breeding grounds for traffic in women, and the trend grew in the twentieth century. Traffickers made use of technological advances like the ocean steamer and the telegraph, which facilitated intercontinental contacts. They sent cables in code, 'offering young lions or brandy', which referred to certain types of girl.[14]

The twentieth century

Soon after the Paris conference the abolitionists achieved their aims in Europe and the United States: in most European countries brothels were closed and state interference with prostitution ended. However, the demand for women's sexual services was not diminished, nor did women stop making a living from prostitution. The two world wars were later to relegate the prostitution problem to the background as sexual virtue was made pointless under the constant pressure of impending death.

After the Second World War, European traffickers sold women to night clubs, brothels and harems in Arabian and African countries. Zanzibar, Mozambique and Angola were the centres of this traffic, which was mainly controlled by Portuguese criminals who had been deported to the African colonies. Their brothels attracted customers from South Africa, where white men were barred from sleeping with black women. After decolonization the market for traffic in Africa dwindled, to be replaced by local networks which supplied women for native men.

Only the traffic in Europe was relatively well documented. In 1965 in Spain Professor Honojosa warned of an agency that was employing girls for jobs abroad but sending them to British and French prostitution rings instead. In Britain, the famous case of Red Max (Max Kassel) hit the headlines. He took girls to Paris only to put them to work on the streets and then left it to his agents to sell them on to brothels in various countries.[15]

The second great case of trafficking in the United Kingdom came to light in 1947. The Messina brothers arrived in Britain after the French had closed down their brothels. They fought the Maltese, who had been trafficking women from Malta. This was small-scale traffic: one man married one woman and put her to work as a prostitute.[16] After the brothers had won their fight with the Maltese, they bought flats throughout London and rented them out to individual girls. Rooms with only one girl were not considered to be brothels, which left the police powerless.

The British authorities did everything they could to prevent the entrance of foreign prostitutes into the country. As they had done in the United States, traffickers resorted to the trick of bogus marriages. An extreme example of this was Etienne Verraud, who managed to contract 27 marriages in only two months. He remained in business for years.[17]

We don't know whether the traffic in women at this time occurred on a large or a small scale. The trade gradually diminished, probably because increasing postwar wealth made women indifferent to false promises of jobs in countries far away. However, an Interpol report in 1965 still listed five main routes:

1   South American women were exported to Puerto Rico, the Mediterranean and the Middle East. Between 1965 and 1974 few cases were recorded of trafficking from Argentina. Some women were recruited from the countryside to be put on the game in Chile, Italy, Turkey and the Middle East.

2　There was a regional market in Europe; for example, French women were sent to German eros centres.[18] As in the 1950s, 1960s and early 1970s there was occasional trafficking between western European countries. A remnant still exists today, usually made up of runaways or addicts who can easily be black-mailed into entering prostitution.

3　European women were sent to developed African countries.

4　There was a regional market in south-east Asia.

5　There were large numbers of foreign prostitutes in Kuwait and Lebanon. Girls from Britain, Germany and France were being held in Beirut.

The Interpol report was based on only a few cases of traffic recorded in each country. Unfortunately the figures are hardly reliable because each government applied its own definition of traffic. Some countries recorded minor concentrations of prosti-tutes as cases of traffic, others merely reported court cases in which pimps were involved. Most countries didn't mention what Interpol called 'disguised traffic in women, the act of hiring women in one country with a view to making them engage in certain types of employment in another country, and in conditions in which they are subjected, incited or exposed to prostitution'. Most people would consider this to be full-blown trafficking. Until the 1970s press coverage of incidents of traffic in European women was very limited.

In 1979 the feminist writer Kathleen Barry brought the issue back into the public eye in her book *Female Sexual Slavery*. She later developed her argument further in *The Prostitution of Sexuality* in 1995. There are some weaknesses in her analysis: for example, she distinguished between voluntary and involuntary slavery, and voluntary slavery is of course a contradiction in terms. She did not differentiate between voluntary and involuntary prostitu-tion. Despite this, Barry's achievement was to get traffic in women a modest place on the United Nations agenda and to have it recognized as an infringement of human rights. At a conference to found an international network against traffic in women Barry said to a journalist that a prostitute:

> may plead for recognition of her work, but it also concerns us. She evokes the image of woman who can be taken. And if you don't take her, you buy her. It is the very basis of rape. Maltreating in marriages, threatening with sexual

violence, prostitution is the red thread of slavery and of taking women hostage.

Barry failed to mention the economic motives for entering prostitution.[19] Her book aroused indignation among prostitutes who considered themselves 'ordinary working girls', but not victims. They pointed out that prostitution could not be ignored in today's society.

The *jungshindae*

Traffic in women has not only been run by organized crime or greedy individuals: governments have also been party to it. Korea was ruled by Japan from 1910 to 1945 and during this time 200,000 Korean women were forced into prostitution to service the Japanese military. The women were known as the *jungshin-dae* – the 'volunteer comforters'. The traffic reached its peak in 1944 when Emperor Hirohito passed the Women's Voluntary Labour Law, which allowed for the systematic procurement of large numbers of Korean women for military brothels.

Often the women were young – the youngest were only eleven and twelve. They were the daughters of farmers ruined by Japanese exploitation, who were promised plenty of good food and money and were often told that they would be working as cooks, domestic helpers or nursing assistants. About a quarter of them died. Those who tried to escape or who caught venereal disease were killed. Many more were massacred as the Japanese army retreated. After the war others were abandoned or offered to the occupying forces. Of those who went back to Korea, many were shunned by their families and forced to change their names. Some committed suicide by jumping off the boat rather than return home.[20]

Some European women who were detained in Japanese concentration camps in south-east Asia during the Second World War were also forced into prositution for the Japanese army. In the 1990s some of them joined with Korean women to sue the Japanese government for compensation.

Sun, sand and sex

Demonstrators against the Vietnam War in the 1960s and early 1970s could hardly have realized that sex tourism would be one of the side effects of peace in south-east Asia. American GIs in the war were often sent to Thailand for R & R (rest and recreation), which added to the existing local market for prostitution in Thailand. After the American soldiers had left, the amusement centres which hosted them lay waste. But not for long. Tour operators found new ways to squeeze money out of the existing infrastructure of bars, discos and massage parlours. Where other strategies of development failed, tourism was a means for Thailand to earn foreign currency. The World Bank and the United Nations both encouraged tourism. In 1991 the proceeds of sex tourism in Thailand amounted to US$3 billion, only 40 per cent of which remained in Thailand. The Thai government had allowed for a limited percentage of non-Thai ownership, but this rule was flouted by the use of puppet heads of companies. The other 60 per cent flowed back into the pockets of European investors. Tourism lured Thai women from the countryside, where they had few prospects, to the tourist centres where they took up prostitution.[21]

The first to explore this market were Japanese men, tired of the professional attitude of Japanese hookers. It was also cheaper to visit prostitutes in Thailand.[22] European travel agencies soon followed suit. Sex tours were organized by both straight tour operators and companies advertising in porno magazines.[23]

The more regular travel agencies didn't flaunt their amenities. They used phrases like 'very suitable for bachelors', or 'sauna and massage available'.[24] Feminists in Europe but particularly in Asia exposed them, demanding that sex tourism be recognized as the racist exploitation of economically weak women. The racism involved in the trade was illustrated by a leaflet advertising Thai women as if they were anthropological specimens: 'When Thai girls are mature, they ask to see the tribal chief: he arranges a sexual rendezvous with their fathers, with compliance of the wives.' This is not true: prostitution is not part of Thai culture. On the contrary, prostitutes are not really accepted. It has to be said, however, that although prostitution is illegal in Thailand, it is tacitly accepted by the government because of the revenue it generates. In most cases Thai prostitutes get to keep only a small part of their earnings; most of the money goes to the sex-tour agencies, the hotels, brothels and bars.[25]

In 1973 the Japanese Women's Christian Temperance Unions described sex tourism as sexual imperialism and succeeded in putting a stop to prostitution in Japan by law.[26] In 1991 sailors from the Gulf arriving at Pattaya in Thailand were welcomed by their wives and families instead of by a bunch of prostitutes. In Europe women demonstrated at airports and forced travel agencies to stop advertising sex tours. A major victory was won in the legal battle with the Norwegian tour operator Ivar Larsen in 1988. This was the first court case ever in the history of sex tourism. His advertising of Thai women in his brochure for his company, Scan Thai Travellers Club, was blatant:

> Thai women don't bother about sexual intimidation as Norwegian women do. Western women consider prostitution as a form of repression whereas Thai women see prostitution as a cultural asset. These dark women are attractive because they are not aware of human rights.
>
> Getting sick of women's rights fanatics – join Scan Thai. Thai women don't strive to be equal to men. On the contrary, it is innate in their culture to serve their husbands.

The Women's Front in Norway learned of Scan Thai and obtained a brochure. They criticized the club for trafficking in women, racism and sexism. Larsen sued Women's Front members in Tonsberg and Oslo for libel. In August 1988 the victory went to the Women's Front and the judge said, 'Generally one must see prostitution as a form of exploitation and oppression of women.'[27]

In the second half of the 1980s other voices were heard, not least those of the Third World prostitutes themselves. They claimed to be dependent on this line of work as their only chance of earning a living. They said their families needed the money because sometimes they were the sole providers.[28]

Traffic to Europe

'I don't have to go all the way to Thailand. Thai girls come here, to the Amsterdam red light district. Besides, I can choose any nationality,' a Dutch punter told me. He's right. The then popularity of underpaid Thai women with sex tourists inspired European brothel-owners to fill their houses with girls from south-east Asia. In 1976 the first oriental 'relax princesses', as they were called, were brought to western Europe; they were often prostitutes who were superfluous to the local and tourist markets.

Similar developments were taking place in Latin America. Tourism to the Dominican Republic, for instance, increased because the currency was devalued against the American dollar. On top of that the Dominican authorities created a favourable tax climate for foreign investors in real estate. In 1990, 3,000 prostitutes were active in the Dominican Republic, catering for both the tourist and local markets.[29] However, there is not always a relationship between sex tourism and traffic. Colombia is a sending country but does not have a fully fledged entertainment industry.

At the start of the 1980s South American women joined their colleagues from south-east Asia; at first it was Colombian and Dominican women in particular who came to Europe. In 1981 the first South American woman with a bought passport arrived at Amsterdam airport.[30] The second group consisted of migrant South American prostitutes recruited by sex bosses: sex-club owners paid commission to procurers.

Now many nationalities, including African and eastern European prostitutes, have entered the scene. Reports have surfaced of women who have been exploited, beaten up, threatened and sometimes raped by traffickers. They have also had to sign contracts for debt bondage. For example: 'You work eleven hours a day. You'll agree to marry for the duration of the contract and you'll end up as a divorcee. Your debt is 15,000 guilders.'[31] Pressure groups who at first opposed sex tourism shifted their attention to the activities of criminal recruiters and were the first to warn of the revival of the trade in women. In 1987 Dutch groups achieved official status for STV, the foundation against traffic in women, when the government agreed to fund it.

3 A global brothel in a global village

Traffic in women is now a global problem. More and more countries are joining the ranks of sending countries, and increasing numbers are becoming target countries. For example Chinese and Burmese women are trafficked to Thailand, Philippine women to Australia and elsewhere, Mexican and Korean women to the United States and Japan, women from the Ivory Coast to France, Brazilian women to Surinam and Austria. The list is far from complete.[1] No country can claim that traffic does not exist within its borders, although some still try to.

Asia

In Asia alone a million people are living in enforced prostitution and slavery.[2] The trafficking of women in Asia is part of a larger picture of development and industrialization. Women destined for western post-industrial countries are usually recruited from regions in developing countries which formerly exported their own produce. Women from the poorest regions, like Bangladesh, are trafficked to developing countries such as India and Pakistan. Within Asia mass migration is going on, especially to the newly industrialized areas. Countries with medium development, such as the Philippines, Taiwan and Korea, are receivers for women from poorer countries like Vietnam, China, Indonesia and Burma. Sending countries are beset by unemployment, chronic poverty, and inability to provide education, medical care or welfare services, as well as by political instability.

When local means of subsistence are swept away by industrialization, the male population moves on to urban areas or abroad, to the Middle East and to countries like Hong Kong and Taiwan, where the economy is booming. However, migrant workers cannot earn enough to support their families because receiving countries are unwilling to pay them reasonable wages. Women migrant workers follow these male population movements. They fill the demand for domestic workers in wealthy families. Other women end up serving tourists and locals in the prostitution market either abroad or in their own country.

The Philippines

Sex tourism is now the third top-dollar earner in the Philippines. In the 1970s, however, it was the largest source of foreign currency. Tourists were sent to prostitution houses in the Ermita-Malata area, or the local tourist belt of Pasay City, Paranaque and Mahati. Many of the bars and brothels were owned by Japanese, Australian or German proprietors. This blatant sex tourism became the target of protests by women's groups, whereupon the tourist agencies moved out to other areas.

Before the US military bases in the Philippines were closed in the early 1990s, there were some 50,000 to 55,000 women servicing the armed forces at the Subic Naval Base in Olongapo City and Clark Air Base in Angeles City.

Malaysia

In Malaysia, a largely Islamic country, sex tourism exists on a modest scale in comparison with Thailand or the Philippines. Currently, there is an influx of women migrants from poorer neighbouring countries. In 1984 more than 200 foreign prostitutes were deported including Filipina and Thai women, who are believed to continue to operate in vice rings across the country. In January 1990 it emerged that an international syndicate had forced several Malaysian girls to work in Japan, Hong Kong, Taiwan and Australia. The women had been promised well-paid jobs, but had ended up in brothels or been stranded in Japan. Many Malaysian children have been reported missing, but they have not been traced to brothels elsewhere.[3]

Taiwan

Women are recruited in the mountain villages and abroad for Taiwan, with its fast-moving economy. Aboriginal mountain people, who form only 1 per cent of the population, are particularly likely to become victims of traffic. In 1986 a Filipino-Chinese man and his Taiwanese wife started to recruit young Filipina women with promises of jobs and marriage to Taiwanese businessmen, who posed as future investors in the Philippines. Filipina women are also trafficked to Hong Kong's sex industry.

India

As many as 200,000 Nepalese prostitutes may be working in India. Yearly, 5,000 to 7,000 Nepalese girls are supposed to be lured into prostitution, for the sex-tourism industry in Katmandu especially, which caters for tourists on 'active sporting holidays'.

Whenever traffic in India is mentioned, the *devadasis* are discussed. These are young girls who are supposed to serve the goddess Yellama by giving themselves, in return for a pittance, to every man who happens to fancy them. Girls destined for this kind of temple service cannot get married but have to be faithful to the goddess. Although it was officially abolished in the late 1970s, the practice is still common, particularly in parts of southern India.

There has been much controversy in women's groups as to whether these girls lived in permanent slavery or enjoyed relative freedom. The German feminist Maria Mies, who has done intensive research in India, claims that some girls would rather be a *devadasi* than a subjugated married woman. Unlike other women, *devadasis* aren't dependent on fathers, brothers or husbands. They pursue a vocational career, partake in religious ceremonies otherwise reserved for men, and have equal inheritance rights with their brothers. On the other hand, during the feudal period they became the slaves of the village overlords, who had the right to deflower them.

Later this religious tradition was capitalized on by Bombay pimps, who bought the girls to use in their brothels. Some 200 girls still end up in Bombay's whorehouses each year. Ordinary girls are also lured from their villages to work in the cities and may find themselves working in the cages in Calcutta's brothels. These are a remnant of British imperialism, when the girls were supposedly caged to protect them from groping Englishmen.

Major cities like New Delhi and Bombay are transit posts for the Gulf region and Pakistan. Like Pakistan, India is a receiving country for women and girls from Bangladesh.[4]

Following immigration towards petrol dollars, the price of women has gone up, to the detriment of the women themselves. This is evident in the size of dowries and brideswealth, the money or goods a groom must pay for his bride. Parents in poorer regions prefer to sell their marriageable daughters to men who have earned something in the boom. On the other hand, in the wealthier Middle East men have been unable to afford the soaring brides-wealth of their nationals and have turned to cheaper brides abroad.

Korea

Nothing is known about North Korea, but South Korea, which is a relatively wealthy country, does have a tradition of traffic in women. Towards the end of the Yi dynasty (1637–1910) wealthy men were entertained by the *kisaeng*, who were high-class courtesans. The *kisaeng* survive in 'entertainment' restaurants, although their status has been diminished. Under the government of Kim Young-Sam these restaurants became meeting places for bribers and bribe takers. The proceeds of economic growth did not flow into manufacturing industry but into the entertainment business. The *nouveau riche* liked to flaunt their wealth in these entertainment restaurants.

Many Korean women who wanted to avoid badly paid factory work tried their luck as waitresses and ended up as *kisaeng*. Their numbers were supplemented by trafficked women from China and the Philippines. In 1988 in Korea 349 official cases of trafficking were recorded, nearly double the figure for 1987. In 1991 a trafficker in custody named 17 large-scale gangs, each procuring an average of 150 women a month, which means that annually 30,000 trafficked women end up in Korea. They are treated badly: women have been burned with cigarette stubs, forcibly tattooed and photographed while being raped. The recruiters, sometimes unlicensed agencies, use universal methods like promises of well-paid jobs. Women have even been kidnapped by people asking directions in the streets, or approached by irresistibly handsome men in parks, 'who want to get to know them better'. The women, who are not as naïve as they may appear, fall for it, because they desperately need the advances they are paid.

Korea is also a sending country. Over 10,000 Korean women work in the Japanese entertainment industry, recruited mostly by fake labour agencies.[5]

China and Hong Kong

Before the communist revolution prostitution in China was part of a whole system of buying and selling women. Young girls were kidnapped or stolen; women were misled by false promises or pawned for adoption, marriage, domestic service or prostitution. Pawning women was common and to have a daughter pawned for prostitution was lucrative, since she could send money home and it was more respectable than selling her. Slavery and prostitution were linked since domestic servants could also be forced into prostitution. Slavery was nominally abolished in China in 1906 and effectively in 1930.[6]

Between 1900 and 1945 people migrated *en masse* from the rural areas to the cities, a development accompanied by major political change. The communist regime gained complete power in 1949 and repressed traffic and prostitution, but with the present liberalization a free market in prostitution is booming. Since state control in rural areas is slackening, scores of women have been trafficked inside China for marriage or prostitution. They are sent to farmers who can't find women to live up to the ideal of the glamorous westernized woman they see on television advertisements. In rural areas, where marriageable women are scarce, it is cheaper to purchase a bride than to pay brideswealth. For example, one woman was picked up by a man in a provincial capital who bought her clothes and took her with him on a business trip. Later on he sold her as a bride to a farmer, who raped her on delivery. She was rescued by the police. In 1992 in the space of a few months 300 traffickers were arrested.[7] The police liberated an estimated 40,000 women and children from slavery.[8] The trafficking problem, now recognized as a major national problem, is acute in Szechuan, a densely populated region where there are thousands of victims. A newspaper reported in 1991 that 65,000 members of 900 gangs were arrested.[9]

'Triads', the gangs which organize Chinese crime including trafficking, originated in a patriotic movement which tried to liberate China from a dictator known as the Manchu Master in the Ch'ing dynasty in the seventeenth century. Over succeeding centuries they aligned themselves with those in power. When Mao Zedong took over in 1949, the army and the triads fled to Hong Kong, Taiwan, southern China and Burma.[10] By the 1980s the Hong Kong triads had grown into syndicates of 800,000 people with a hard-core membership of 80,000. Hong Kong has only 6 million inhabitants.[11]

Traffic in girls to Europe occurs against the background of China's one-child policy. Parents prefer boys and don't know what to do with their superfluous daughters. Boys are trafficked to parents who only have girls.[12] One future trend may well be the large-scale trafficking of Chinese girls to Europe. Because Hong Kong transfers to China in 1997, Hong Kong criminals are moving into Europe. Gangs are trafficking people for various purposes, such as slavery in restaurants[13] and, it is suspected, exploitation in households and private brothels. Reports of young Chinese girls being sold are common. As a rule they have been brought to Europe by elderly men and a few are promised political asylum. Chinese gangs promise the girls they will search for their families abroad.

Japan

'Are you no taller than 1 metre, 72 centimetres?' the man on the telephone asked when I called about an advertisement for a waitress in a night club in Japan which appeared in Dutch newspapers in 1994. In Japan they don't like tall girls. When I contacted it, the Japanese embassy expressed great doubt about the advertisement's reliability. For a foreigner it is next to impossible to get a work permit for Japan. STV received many calls from worried mothers whose daughters wanted to go there after seeing the advertisement. After all Japan has a high standard of living and many European girls and women face unemployment. So far there are no reports from women who have come back.

Japan's entertainment market is the territory of Japanese organized crime, the yakuza, and they have controlled it since the 1940s. The American occupying forces after the Second World War westernized the Japanese prostitution scene. Traditional geishas were relegated to the background and the yakuza, which had prospered on the black market, procured prostitutes for the American forces.

Japan became industrialized in the 1960s. The standard of living rose and the yakuza concentrated on luxury, amusement, real estate, drugs and prostitution.[14] In the mid-1970s they became active in south-east Asia and took up sex tourism.[15] Now they have strongholds in Thailand, the Philippines and other Asian countries. The influential yakuza boss, 'oyabun' Kodama, who was a great friend of President Marcos of the Philippines, helped his former cellmate, Ryoichi Sasakawa, to set up in sex tourism. In 1979 Sasakawa tried to buy the island of Lubang and transform it into a sex ghetto. However, he was stopped by the churches and by women's groups. After protests the yakuza abandoned sex tourism and concentrated on large-scale traffic in women. In the 1980s they recruited the first Philippine women for Japan's sex industry.

When Japanese sex tourism to the Philippines declined due to competition, many Philippine women went to Japan to work and quite often ended up in the entertainment industry.[16]

The yakuza boast of their sixteenth-century origin and still retain remnants of their long history in their feudal organization and physical characteristics, such as tattoos and hacked-off little fingers.[17] The yakuza have 100,000 members, divided between 29 clans. Although the younger generation of the yakuza rebel, the organization is still strictly hierarchical. New members have to undergo three years of physical and mental ascetic training.

Australasia

'Nothing ever happens in Australia, apart from the occasional bushfire. So you can't blame people for joking about sheep and kangaroos,' an Australian prostitute said to me. Still, Australia has its own part to play in the international trafficking in women. It is mentioned occasionally as a target country for dancers to work in yakuza-controlled Japanese night clubs, but it is also a receiving country in the marriage introduction racket. Nowadays Australia constitutes the biggest market for brides, who are taken to isolated mining and cattle towns. Marriage agencies are disguised as organized tours and pen-friend organizations and their fees are between A\$300 and A\$1,000. The women are profiled in magazines and on videotape. One agency manager claims he only has to go to the market square to find a bevy of Filipinas ready to be videotaped.

A so-called serial husband, who tastes and discards one bride after another, Kenneth Morgan, sparked off nationwide protest with his book published in the 1980s extolling the meek Filipina dream wife (most mail-order brides in Australia come from the Philippines). Serial husbands are often much older and worse educated than their future wives and 10 per cent of these marriages end in divorce. When asked why she wanted to marry such a husband, one Filipina answered, 'Well, he has definite and concrete plans in life.' Marriage services connecting Filipinas to Australians started up in the late 1960s and early 1970s.

Generally the Filipinos figure in the top 20 nationalities emigrating to Australia and since 1974 the majority have been women. At first highly trained Filipinas arrived, then in 1977 there was a large influx of women who were mainly brides, which led the authorities to restrict immigration. In 1983 it was cut back further. The prevalence of Filipinas marrying Australians is four times higher than in Canada and three times that in the United States.[18]

The Australian Lower House has declared the practice of matching foreign women to Australian men by mail order reprehensible and proposed a six-month penalty on the practice. The bill has not yet come into force.

There is little information on trafficking in New Zealand, but Thai women in particular work in the brothels there on tourists' visas.

The United States

The USA seems to be the country furthest from recognizing the problem of traffic in women. At the beginning of the twentieth century it joined the global outcry against traffic[19] and Congress passed the Mann and Bennet Acts prohibiting interstate and international traffic. After strict immigration laws were passed in 1924 international traffickers were supposed to have lost interest in the country. The USA still basks comfortably in the idea that trafficking doesn't exist within its boundaries.

However, in the mid 1980s a marriage racket came to light, involving American soldiers who had married Korean women, run by an organization of mafia-like proportions with tentacles in New York, Philadelphia and Houston. The men were paid $10,000 for their inconvenience. Army sources reveal that annually 20,000 Americans return from Korea. In 1985 2,777 Americans married Korean women; 90 per cent of the Korean prostitutes in the United States are wives or ex-wives of American soldiers. In the first half of 1986 there were 1,044 American-Korean marriages. The Immigration and Naturalization Service vetted some 300 soldiers who had married and divorced Korean women in the preceding three years. Only three American soldiers were convicted of arranging bogus marriages and black market activities. After these cases American GIs have had to sign a document stating that they are aware they can be punished if they engage in the marriage racket.[20]

Since the fall of the Berlin Wall in 1989, a new, highly organized market has burgeoned: the commercial pairing of Russian and other eastern European women with American suitors. An agency called American Russian Matchmaking produces a catalogue advertising 20,000 candidate wives. The women have to pay up to US$80 to join the agency, twice as much as their future American partners. The men, however, have to pay a considerable sum for a Russian tour on which they meet a selection of three Russian women. As a bonus, if a decision is reached within 48 hours the agency provides the woman with a two-year conditional visa. If she decides to leave her husband before that time, she will be deported.[21]

On 9 March 1993, the American cable company CNN broadcast a rare item on traffic in women in the USA. It was not specified where the women came from, but it stands to reason that Mexican women are smuggled into the country for prostitution purposes. In 1993 it was also established that many Latin American women have been introduced to unmarried American men. Agencies catered for men who had divorced their liberated wives.

'Besides a large number of mail-order brides from Thailand and other women from Third World countries there are many migrants working here as sex workers,' says Priscilla Alexander of the National Task Force on Prostitution. 'They are trafficked to the extent that they can't get visas. In New York there are also many women from the Dominican Republic. I don't know how they migrate but they are known as women who make many phone calls, presumably to people they have to pay, possibly their families. They have to find the money to get here. Many have forged documents in some way or another because they can't get visas. They pay ridiculously high sums for their airfares, from US$5,000 to US$6,000, which is too much. It really costs far less. They travel around. Many South American women work in Mexican brothels. In Chiapas you have legal and illegal brothels. Only Mexican women work in legal brothels, but in the illegal brothels you have women from other Latin American countries. I know a woman who has been there, and she seemed to think they worked voluntarily.

'There must be trafficked women in Chinatowns. Recently after two raids Chinese women were taken out of a New York brothel where they were held captive. They were not released until they had handed over the proceeds of 200–300 customers, as their contracts stated. And these contracts could be sold to other brothels.

'There are many Thai women working in massage parlours. I imagine some of them have gone through the same thing, but I don't think they are willing to talk about it. They traffic themselves.'

To European eyes these sex workers are migrants who will do anything to get into the United States. They know what they want and they have to pay to get it.

Africa

Little is known about traffic inside Africa, but there is evidence that many African women are brought into Europe on false papers. They are afraid of the authorities because most of them have bought their false documents on the streets, for example in Ghana. The first incident of smuggled Ghanaians in the Netherlands, for example, was reported in 1982; but the Criminal Intelligence Unit has no reported cases of trafficked Ghanaian women. Leen Pieterse of the Unit and of Interpol said, 'We can't tell if they work voluntarily or not. Ghanaian women commute between Düsseldorf and Aachen. In Italy and Belgium there are quite a few women from Ghana and other African countries.'

A Dutch madam who employs them said, 'Of course you can't meet African women. They fear outsiders because they are illegal. Some of them are forced to peddle drugs at the airport. One Ghanaian woman applied to my call-girl company, but she told me she had to telephone home every hour. Besides, she had to account to a godmother who lived in Germany.'

'There are many girls from Ghana working in the same joint as me,' a Dutch prostitute told me. 'I know they all come via Belgium. They all claim to have a brother as a business partner. As far as I can see, these so-called brothers are ordinary pimps.' These men also pass themselves off as future husbands.

It is striking how many African women apply to Payoke, the Belgian organization for prostitutes' rights and support for trafficked women, for help.[22] Formerly they were recruited for the marriage racket: in 1985 there was a sharp increase in marriages between Belgians and Ghanaian or Nigerian women; even residents of old people's homes were marrying to provide trafficked women with Belgian nationality. Now African women are entering Belgium on false applications for political asylum. Between February 1988 and November 1992, 2,859 Nigerians were registered, among whom were many women who later surfaced in prostitution.[23]

In November 1993 a network of 43 traffickers and victims from Nigeria, Liberia and the Ivory Coast was exposed. In exchange for false documents the women had handed in their own passports, which were then used for other people. The traffickers were charged with procuring false documents, profiting from prostitution, embezzlement and organizing criminal activities. The victims were also rounded up for using false papers, being complicit in fraud and working as prostitutes. The African women were too afraid to talk at the trial; those who did were considered traitors. One woman asked to be brought into court handcuffed to give the impression that she was one of the accused. The case was complicated by the women's fear of a kind of voodoo: they were convinced they could be harmed from a great distance.

Ghanaian women also enter Europe by way of Italy. Nigerians move about, whereas Ghanaian women stay in their clans.[24] In Italy they pay their debts via African middlemen and avoid the police because they feel more secure paying off their debts.[25] In 1989 and 1990 5,000 Nigerian women were working in Italy as prostitutes, most of whom were trafficked, according to Interpol. The police tried to close down the brothels where they worked, but the women bricked up the windows because they were afraid they would be repatriated.[26]

Western Europe

Belgium

Antwerp, early in the morning. The red light district, where window prostitution has long been housed, looks bleak. Bars are up for sale, hotels look dilapidated. It is cold. Only one black woman is at work. In the centre of the district Payoke has its office. There they told me that one of the many problems in the neighbourhood is monopoly formation by the Dutch and German underworld. Dutch owners divide the studio spaces into smaller units, as they do in the Netherlands. Gangs from former Yugoslavia join by using nominal owners and Albanian criminals are now making nuisances of themselves.

'The district is a hotbed of criminality; that is to say, trade in drugs, arms and women,' one of the workers at Payoke told me. Another staff member took me on a tour. On our way we met Tanya, who was recruited by the Georgian mafia. A member of the mafia, who owned a store in Antwerp, was still free and using his many contacts in the area. In 1993 Payoke helped 88 trafficked women, among whom were many from the Philippines, Africa and Hungary.

Belgium has a policy for victims of traffic similar to that operating in the Netherlands and Germany. They are allowed to remain in the country for 45 days without having to press charges. They are entitled to a permit to stay for three months, which can be renewed every four months, when charges are brought. They get a permanent residence permit when their case has been heard in court. Belgium is unique, however, because victims of traffic other than for prostitution purposes are recognized. The late King Baudouin devoted a lot of his energies to combating trafficking. In recognition of his concern with the problem, a victim spoke about trafficking in front of the assembled heads of state at his funeral.

Germany

'At first we didn't want to recognize the problem of traffic in women. If prostitution is labour, why shouldn't labour agencies be legal? But when we heard stories about women being beaten up and dying from asphyxiation in the containers they were smuggled in, we changed our point of view,' Helga from Hydra, one of Germany's prostitutes' rights movement, said at a conference on traffic in women.

Germany has a history of tolerating prostitution in certain exclusive areas, such as the eros centres. In the 1960s these attracted Austrian criminals who had become unemployed when Austria closed its brothels. At first traffic seemed two-way between Germany and Austria, but rivalry ensued and the Austrians left to set up organizations in other countries.[27] Later on, when the centre of traffic in women collapsed in the Lebanon because of the civil war, a new generation of traffickers turned their attention to Germany.[28] In Germany there are now several organizations which help trafficked women and discuss the problem theoretically, one of which is AGISRA (Arbeitsgemeinschaft Gegen Internationale Sexuelle und Rassistische Ausbeutung).

Some 75 per cent of Germany's prostitutes are foreigners. In Frankfurt they are mostly Latin American. Women from Uruguay and Argentina were taken through Germany to be married in Italy. It is difficult to explain why so many women from Paraguay work in Germany when hardly any do in the Netherlands. Josephina from Colombia said, 'When I was working in German prostitution, many prostitutes from Brazil and Uruguay were controlled by Italian pimps. In Germany Italians, Uruguayans and Argentinians worked together with German pimps. Many women from Paraguay working in Germany are married to Italian pimps. I don't know why these particular groups worked together but I guess they already did that in South America.'

In Germany traffic for arranged marriages is rife. In one notorious case a member of a bowling club married an Asian woman to share her with his club mates. In the late 1980s the authorities imposed a crackdown on bogus marriages, which were the way most Thai girls entered prostitution. In some German states women who report trafficking can remain in the country for a variable period of time.

Before 1993, 517 incidences of traffic in women were recorded in Germany, but that number should be treated with caution. Not all the cases were properly documented; for example, German victims of pimps were also included. As in other European countries, there is a striking increase in the number of cases involving Russian and other eastern European women.

Between January 1992 and December 1993, 911 victims of traffic were reported, one of them male; 286 of the women had never worked in prostitution and did not realize they would end up on the game; 192 women knew what it all was about. What the other 433 expected is unknown. Many of the suspected traffickers, 32.8 per cent, were from former Yugoslavia and the eastern European countries. Turkish traffickers were also well represented at 17.7 per cent; and 329 out of the 777 were German nationals. Fourteen Italians and seven Greeks also plied their trade in Germany. They used the familiar methods of recruitment: promises of jobs as cooks, domestic workers, nannies, dancers, waitresses or models. Many of the victims were addressed personally or contacted via advertisements. Most women travel overland, the easiest and cheapest route to Germany. In some parts of the country trafficked women can legally await the trial of their traffickers.

Switzerland

Women working in Switzerland come from Thailand, the Philippines, South Korea, Brazil, Colombia, the Dominican Republic, Haiti, Ghana, Kenya and eastern European countries.[29] Switzerland has a tradition of exploiting entertainers. In 1981 the first complaints were lodged against traffickers. The Swiss Association of Erotic Companies claimed that these women, who were often recruited at beauty contests, were free to go where they liked and were in fact better off than Swiss prostitutes.[30] In 1987 the Swiss authorities issued only seven entertainers' visas, whereas in 1991 the number had risen to 269. These go-go dancers are employed with a variety of dubious contracts. A stripper has to pay her own way home, usually with earnings from prostitution. Most women arriving from abroad don't know that dancing means *strip intégral*, or completely naked. The Swiss police often don't bother to check on the person who is standing guarantor for a woman entering the country. Only when they arrive does the agency decide whether or not the women are fit for the job; if they are accepted, they can dance for eight months. If their contracts are extended, the women have to leave the country for four months before they can return. As a rule they don't go home but turn to prostitution in neighbouring countries because no other employment is open to them. Their contracts have to be ratified by the foreigners' police, but even so they can be fired within the first three days. They have no insurance cover.[31]

The United Kingdom

'Philippine models, Spanish beauties, call 0171–' reads a typical card on the walls of a London phone booth. However, the UK is conspicuously absent from all reports of traffic in women for the prostitution market. Because of the UK's geographical situation it is not easy to smuggle people into the country. The people brought in illegally are usually males. However, many methods of recruitment for traffic could still work in the United Kingdom. Jean Gould, a London solicitor, said, 'Rich families offer to take a girl of a poor family to Europe and to pay for her education, as some Nigerians do. Sometimes these girls are brought in under a false name. I have handled two cases. The second girl travelled on the papers of the first girl. Some Latin Americans pull the trick of artificial family connections [see chapter 7]. It is also possible to issue a phoney invitation to work with a British firm as a translator or "public relations manager". An employer in one of the cases was prosecuted for faking evidence. We don't know if these girls are exploited in prostitution.'

Small-scale traffic certainly exists in Britain. But how about large-scale trade in women? John Deal of New Scotland Yard answered my query, 'To my knowledge it does not happen.' He referred me to Chief Inspector Spencer of the Crime Committee, who said, 'I am not qualified to comment upon that. Illegal immigrants are the concern of the Home Office. Suppose large-scale traffic in women occurred in the United Kingdom, the women would be rounded up as prostitutes in the first place. If it were organized or serious crime, it would be investigated in a different way. We are conscious of developments on the continent with eastern European crime, but that is all I can say.'

Under UK law it is unlikely that anyone will come forward to denounce traffickers. The Sexual Offences Act makes it a crime to work as a prostitute or to use an office to bring women into prostitution, as in call-girl agencies, for example. According to the Street Offences Act it is illegal to loiter and to solicit. A law dating from 1985 criminalizes punters, because 'it was not considered fair and emancipated just to arrest the women'. The result is that customers are wary, but are hardly ever arrested. Because of these laws the English Collective of Prostitutes (ECP) will never invoke the help of the police to prevent traffic in women. 'All prostitution laws work against prostitutes. A strengthening of the police powers only worsens the position of migrant women. We don't want any licensing of brothels. You can't equate licensing with decriminalization. State brothels did nothing to better the position of women in the past. Licensing brothels could give traffickers a chance; they can invest big money and put their own people in. We see little evidence of trafficking in women. It might occur with women who work in massage parlours. We do know women who work for individual pimps. Black and migrant women are working on the streets where they suffer the most violence. The premises are controlled by people who don't want black people working there. Any legalization affects migrant women.

'The police don't use the law to arrest violent pimps, but to break up the relations of prostitutes, to criminalize men. They don't arrest the real pimps. It might be a good thing to have a crackdown on procuring when violence or force is involved, but in England a prostitute's mother can be accused if she accepts a drink from her daughter in a pub.

'In England organized crime is just an excuse to arrest prostitutes. The police consider hookers' flats hotbeds of organized crime. The police organize crime themselves. When we were occupying a church to protest against indiscriminate arrests of women, they sided with the pimps who were waiting outside.'

The English Collective of Prostitutes is housed in Camden Town, near King's Cross, a well-known area for kerb-crawling. Niki Adams and Nina Lopez of the ECP freely hand out information in a room lined with old books on feminism, Marxism and household work. They are also associated with the campaign to recognize housework as official labour.

Walking through Gerrard Street in London's Chinatown, it is hard to believe that this friendly area is a hotbed of forced prostitution, but a few years ago the BBC broadcast a disquieting documentary on the role of the triads in this crime. The area attracts many Londoners and tourists to its well-supplied supermarkets and restaurants and caters for some 300,000 Chinese people scattered throughout the capital. Amidst the bustle the Chinese Community Centre is a haven for Chinese people who want to read a paper or a book. 'That documentary was a bit overdone,' one of the Centre's workers said, 'but prostitution is taboo in the Chinese community. Here the triads are not as big as in Hong Kong. People are scared. The police could not protect the victims. I was hurt when I heard triads do in fact exist in London, but, touch wood, they have not come to the Community Centre. In London they are busy loan-sharking. Recently they threatened an old lady and took away her passport. Now they are recruiting youngsters.

'We have not come across traffic in women, but there are many domestic workers from mainland China. They are really exploited, they live in laundries and get tuberculosis. The Chinese people in England are originally from Hong Kong. Most Chinese people work in catering and that doesn't take place in secrecy. We are the fifth generation: the first Chinese came to England less than a century ago as sailors. They gathered in Tower Hamlets and started a laundry. In the 1960s, 98 per cent of the Chinese community in England worked in catering. They needed wives to help them run their takeaways. They had no days off. Families joined them. The children were not well educated and could not catch up with English children because of language problems. The parents just worked hard. Wives came over and were promised a better life. They worked long hours and lived isolated lives. They were not exactly cheated, but England was not what they had expected. Women in arranged marriages were not happy. Gambling was the only way out for these migrants. It still is. Drinking is also a problem. Families suffer from these problems. They ask old friends to borrow money. Old people are reluctant to accept benefit, because they are afraid of losing face.

'Chinese women may now seek better employment and come here on tourist visas. They also come here for political reasons. They come as a student or to seek asylum. They may find employment on the black market.'

Eastern Europe

Czech Republic

Hana Malinová is the expert on prostitution in the Czech Republic. She is a street-corner worker for the country's only organization for prostitutes. She described the situation there at a conference in Prague. 'Before the Velvet Revolution in 1989 a free market existed for commercial sex. Many hookers served tourists in the big hotels. They made good money. High-class prostitutes also took up positions at the airport. At the time middle-class prostitutes tried to make a fortune in places where local men gathered. Cheap hookers, usually runaways or mentally retarded women, were to be found at the large railway stations.

'Under communism everybody, including whores, had to register their livelihood on their identity papers. People without a job invariably were saddled with a criminal record, and when a woman couldn't prove she had an acceptable profession, she was sent straight to jail. There she mixed with women who had committed serious crimes like murder. That's why at the time most prostitutes paid to have themselves registered as cleaners in hotels. These regulations to combat "parasitism" were abolished after the Velvet Revolution.

'There were pimps under communism. They were mostly black-market money changers who worked as taxi drivers and porters at the big hotels. They had regular contact with both tourists and prostitutes and exchanged foreign currency for the hookers. Quite a few of them joined the mafia.

'After the Velvet Revolution prostitution became a booming business. The fall of the Berlin Wall stimulated a type of sex tourism, especially to the border regions, but not in Prague. In the capital sex tourists only have a limited choice. Brothels aren't easy to find because the women working there are keen to protect their territory from competition from outsiders. Most tourists in the border regions are truckers and men who travel on their own, many of them Germans who live near the border. They tell their wives they cross the border just to have a cheap meal, but instead of eating they pick up a girl. Once I took a woman to see where her husband was going to eat. She took it badly.

'There is enough room for streetwalkers along the thoroughfares in the border regions. But it is next to impossible to secure a place without help. The girls are supposed to hand over a part of their earnings to the person who has paid for their place in the line.

'There are many female pimps, who focus especially on young girls. In the border regions many gypsy families are actively involved in the trade in women. These families welcome the girls, who appreciate it because they are very isolated. They are usually runaways from broken homes who can't go back. Since they avoid outsiders, it is very difficult to get a hold on these trafficking gypsy communities.

'Women are sold on into Germany. Their papers are arranged in a few days by the Yugoslavian criminals operating there. The Czech mafia is dominated by German and Bulgarian criminal organizations. Abductions constitute a major problem, but the women don't or won't talk about it. Some girls are so afraid of kidnapping that they hardly dare to go to the lavatory. It is not uncommon for the women to be filled with alcohol before they are pushed into cars to go to Germany. Rumour has it that in the last couple of years 8,000 girls have disappeared in this way. However, we have been unable to confirm that figure.

'It is easy for traffickers to convince the women to work abroad. Some agree to work as prostitutes, provided the working conditions are reasonable. They see it as a temporary solution to their problems. Specialized travel agencies distribute them to Italy and Greece,' Hana concluded.

Slovakia

I also spoke to a Slovakian expert, Gabriel Bianchi, who gave a lecture on the situation in his country. 'In Slovakia's border region there is a lot of prostitution. The Russian mafia have infiltrated. Their only problem is that the women have few clients. There is not a big market for prostitution in Slovakia.

'Professional prostitutes are soliciting in hotels. Bars are the domain of less professional women. Besides street prostitutes, there are "guestworkers", women who live close to the border and go to Austria to work for the weekend. Bratislava is only 100 kilometres from Budapest and 60 from Vienna. Street prostitution in Austria is almost entirely an eastern European affair.'

Poland

'I was fired under communism because I insisted that prostitution did in fact exist in Poland,' said the Polish lawyer Sylvia Igra. Sylvia and 14 Polish women from the YWCA (Young Women's Christian Association) and the Polish Feminist Association participated in a seminar about prostitution and traffic in women in the Netherlands in 1994. Sylvia said, 'Up to now prostitution in Poland has not been forbidden and hookers are not registered with the police. Communists have always denied the existence of commercial sex in a workers' paradise. What doesn't exist, cannot be forbidden.'

Barbara Limanowska of the Polish Feminist Association said, 'Until 1991 the Polish prostitution market was stable. But then peepshows and massage parlours appeared on the scene. Now most women work in sex clubs and escort services. There are over 100 escort agencies in Warsaw alone. There is also prostitution in fast-food restaurants, and part-time prostitution and juvenile prostitution in the border region.' Prostitution is not just for tourists any more. The Russian mafia have taken over and Poland is a target country for traffic in women. However, many Russian prostitutes come voluntarily to Poland. They can enter Poland when they have enough zlotys to last their stay. They befriend Polish hookers, who put them up. The police don't intervene because it happens in private homes. Only when the neighbours complain about the public nuisance do the police come to deport the women. The press interprets this as Russian women liking the job better than Polish girls. In fact 12 per cent of the women working in Poland are foreigners.

Beata Fiszer, also from the Association, pointed out that the Polish media suggest that women become victims of traffic voluntarily. 'Polish women are beautiful, and that's why they are being sold,' is what reporters want to hear.

Tina Wieruszewska founded an organization for missing children after her daughter and her friend went missing without trace in 1992. Only the girls' passports were recovered. Tina asked Interpol and no fewer than 20 embassies for help. She questioned whether the police took the case seriously.

Wieslawa Stzylkowska, who co-ordinates all investigations of traffic in women in Poland at Warsaw police headquarters, was also at the 1994 conference: 'Unlike the government, the Polish police have done much to prevent and fight traffic in women. We work together with Interpol.'[32] In 1993, 44 cases of trafficking in women were brought to court. 'There is a direct line of trafficking from Poland to Germany and hence to the Netherlands and Belgium. Traffickers are assisted by Turkish bar owners in Germany. Polish men sell women to German club owners for 2,000–3,000 marks. The women are covered with blankets to hide them from custom officers. There is much traffic for marriage as well as for prostitution.'

4 Traffic and prostitution in the Netherlands

Crocodiles of tourists move through the famous red light district in Amsterdam, the women with their handbags safely tucked under their arms. A sightseeing boat passes by on the canal. Angrily the window prostitutes close their curtains.

'Nowhere is prostitution practised as openly as here.' Conchita from the Dominican Republic told me that this was her first impression when she saw her future workplace. Amidst the bustle she is silent and subdued. The people who accompanied her to the Netherlands have just told her she can only work as a prostitute. Up till now Conchita had believed she would be working in a beauty parlour.

The easiest way to save Conchita and her fellow victims might seem to be to close down all brothels. This policy was tried throughout Europe, including the Netherlands, at the turn of the century, but to no avail. Prostitution was driven underground, only to resurface conspicuously in the following decades. When the licensed brothels were shut, the sex trade in the Netherlands was carried on behind the façades of boarding houses, the future window brothels. Prostitution became a thriving business and the authorities saw no alternative to tolerating it.

In the 1960s the sex business had to operate in a situation in which prostitution was not the only source of extramarital sex. With widespread use of the contraceptive pill promiscuity became less risky, and sexually transmitted diseases were easily treatable with antibiotics. The controllers of prostitution reacted by creating sex clubs, where men could relax with girls. The numbers of these clubs, featuring new gadgets such as whirlpools and private porno cabins, mushroomed in the 1970s. By the end of the 1980s prostitution was no longer a surreptitious marginal trade, but was

41

openly integrated into the service sector. In the clubs sex became a recreational indoor activity.

The normalization of prostitution

In the 1970s the Dutch authorities decided to tolerate prostitution. They adopted the position that if some people are willing to sell sex and others are prepared to pay for it, the law has no reason to intervene. The government still banned the promotion of prostitution and living off a prostitute by a third party. There is a flaw in this liberal attitude, however, in that a third party is necessary to organize a place where clients and prostitutes can meet. If you tolerate prostitutes, you also have to tolerate brothel-owners. The result was that many prostitutes had to rely on illegal entrepreneurs for a place where they could work. To overcome this, it was suggested that the article in the penal code forbidding the organization and promotion of prostitution be abolished. Prostitution would therefore be legalized in all but name. The argument continues. Prostitution in the Netherlands is still not formally legalized, but will be early in 1996.

In the 1980s the demand for legalization was accompanied by a campaign to recognize prostitution as labour. This was initiated by prostitutes, supported by a small group of feminists. At that time there were three main feminist views on prostitution. The first saw it as sexual violence. Feminist hookers, on the other hand, believed that prostitution is a vocation in which women can explore their sexuality, and their feminist supporters stated that the stigma of whore was put on all women who didn't obey male rules ('Good girls go to heaven, bad girls go everywhere,' was one of their sayings). A third group recognized prostitution as labour, but as disagreeable labour undertaken from economic necessity.[1]

Through discussion of these views an official policy was eventually reached, which stated that on grounds of sexual autonomy women from all countries have the right to work as a prostitute and the right to refuse to work as a prostitute. Coercion and exploitation should be prevented. As a result working conditions, which were generally bad, became an issue in the prostitutes' rights movement.

Professional prostitutes resented the large sums, 40 to 60 per cent of their earnings, which they had to pay to brothel-keepers. Window prostitutes were no better off. To rent a window for one night costs the same as a night in the Hilton Hotel. However, window prostitutes can at least choose their working hours. Whether a prostitute is a high-class call girl or working the windows, she makes on average £15 an hour before tax. Prostitutes have no free health insurance, paid sick leave or holidays.

The recruitment of foreign prostitutes

Brothel-owners and managers enforce rules which no other employer would dare to. The women have to clean their workplace and do striptease without pay. In some houses women are fined if they are five minutes late. Dutch prostitutes discovered they could make more money working from their own homes. The result was a continual shortage of staff in clubs because of the high turnover of women. Managers no longer wanted to employ emancipated prostitutes in their joints and solved the problem by recruiting women from 'low-wage' countries.[2]

Brothel-keeper Ron W. said to a newspaper, 'It became increasingly difficult to make these Dutch hookers toe the line. Due to emancipation they have become too dominant ... my joint looked more like a feminist shelter than a brothel. In that respect the latinas were a relief. They worked like racehorses, and never nagged because they didn't speak the language.'[3]

Eventually the Third World women proved not to be docile enough, so the managers turned to eastern Europe. In 1992, after the fall of the Berlin Wall, the manager of a brothel was reported as saying in a local newspaper, 'Now nine out of ten women working here are from eastern European countries. Dutch and German women are all drug addicts, and those chicks from the Dominican Republic became too cheeky after a while.'[4]

The owners of window brothels also replaced demanding and independent women with submissive women. A Dutch prostitute who took me on a tour around the Amsterdam red light district complained, 'It as an outrage how foreign women are exploited. Sometimes they have to pay more for their windows than Dutch prostitutes, while migrants are allotted the dirtiest rooms.' She pointed out studio spaces no bigger than telephone kiosks, which looked like the crates in which animals are kept. 'The owners of these houses split up these rooms time and again. They only think of pocketing more rent. They have six women sleeping in one room.'

Most foreign women are horrified when they see these places for the first time. Those who voluntarily become prostitutes mistakenly believe that the life of a prostitute in the Netherlands is one of glamour, drinking champagne in a smart dress. A Colombian woman said, 'In Bogotá I thought that in the Netherlands I was going to work in a club with a swimming pool. But I had to work in a small room. There is not even time to talk to the customers. They send you straight to bed.' While women who have legal status in the Netherlands vote with their feet and find another brothel or quit prostitution, brothel-keepers can easily exploit illegal immigrants, trafficked or not, who are under pressure to earn money for their families. 'Dutch women don't have to do this work. They speak the language, are well educated and can choose,' said Conchita, one of the trafficked women.

The punters

Like any other industry prostitution is subject to the market forces of supply and demand. With this in mind, it has been suggested that the punters should be called on to boycott exploited women. When the first planeloads of foreign women arrived it was thought they would cater for clients with exotic tastes, but this was later disproved when eastern European women arrived who don't look exotic at all. Client Gerrit, one of the few punters who spoke openly to me about his visits to prostitutes, said, 'It is not true there suddenly was a market for black women. There is a demand for cheap prostitutes. For a few quid you can find a nice Latin American woman. I often visit prostitutes and I don't want to pay too much. Only language is a problem. Foreign women don't charge extra for special services, like Dutch women do. They only make me pay for the time I spend with them. They are also less sophisticated. I can tell from the way they ask me whether I want to use a condom that they are willing to go without once in a while.'

Many foreign women are used to a different style of prostitution. In their home countries they can establish relationships with a client for a whole evening. Josephina from Colombia said, 'Not all foreign women work cheaply. I for one charged normal prices and never went without a condom. The punters want everything for nothing, they are part of the cause of exploitation of foreign prostitutes.' Some clients extort money from prostitutes by posing as a policeman, doctor or lawyer, assuming that illegal immigrants won't dare to question their authority.

Increase in trafficking

The number of prostitutes in the Netherlands, including part-timers, is estimated to be around 30,000. About a third come from countries outside the European Union, and this figure rises to 50 per cent in the major cities.

In a raid in which illegal immigrants are detained, some 20 per cent of them won't have a passport or will hint at financial obligations to a third party. Even if these women are not clear victims of trafficking, they have been helped by profiteers or middlemen, or promised marriage in return for money. Most eastern European women have a 'friend' for whom they work, but whether this is voluntary is unclear. Some women prefer to negotiate for more money themselves rather than contact the police or a social worker. Some want to continue working because their meagre earnings exceed the salary they can earn in a normal job in their home country.

On average 100 new cases of traffic a year are reported to STV. In 1994 this number rose to 170. Each of these women knows on average three other trafficked women. If the number of victims of trafficking already present in the Netherlands is included, then it can be estimated that there are at least 1,000 trafficked women in one small country.

Cases which altered Dutch law

A striking example of an active, campaigning 'victim' was Lisa from the Philippines, who made her case into a public issue. Her story is as follows. Her situation in the Philippines was difficult. One day she met a local chief prosecutor, who promised her a job as a receptionist in a Dutch hotel owned by a friend of his. She accepted and in October 1981 went to the Netherlands. There she was forced into prostitution in a so-called sex farm. She had to repay an enormous debt, some £10,000. A local farmer met her as a client and rescued her. At first the authorities refused to believe his stories about Lisa's condition. Then Lisa took action. She was brave enough to address a Dutch parliamentary hearing on trafficking in women on 14 September 1987 in a spectacular session. She said among other things, 'What I want to ask you politicians today is this: why does the Dutch government not do anything to stop this terrible thing which is going on everywhere?

'I think that the Dutch Ministry of Justice does not understand what this does to women who become victims. What happened to me is very clear. What more do you want? I feel more like the accused than a victim, having to defend myself when I have done nothing wrong.'

Lisa did not leave the matter there. In 1988 she joined a rogatory commission, an investigatory committee of the Department of Justice and the police which went to the Philippines, where her Dutch recruiter was hiding. A television company made a documentary of this search, which shocked the nation. The Dutch recruiter was found guilty. In 1990 she took her case to the Philippines to bring the man who recruited her and misled her in the first place to trial. The case against him failed. Before retiring disappointed, in 1990 she received the Marga Klompé Award for her courage and persistence. At the award ceremony she said, 'It is especially nice to be here, when I think that my life was almost ruined. I was deceived and sold by a fellow Filipino and then exploited by a Dutch trafficker. Already for more than seven years I have been struggling, fighting for my rights and to get the guilty ones punished. I am proud to say that my fight has achieved something for myself and other women.'

One result of Lisa's evidence was that after 1987 all victims of traffic in women who want to lodge a complaint are entitled to a temporary residence permit. They can now stay legally in the Netherlands during the police investigations and the subsequent trial. Formerly it was next to impossible to bring traffickers to trial because the police, after discovering the victims were illegal aliens, deported them immediately.[5]

Lisa was not the only trafficked woman to have an impact on Dutch government policy. Once the threat of immediate expulsion was removed, fear of reprisals came to the fore. This was evident in the case of the Colombians, which is described in chapter 6. These women had been so badly threatened that they did not dare to tell the whole story. 'After I had spoken to the police for the first time, the traffickers let me know I'd better be careful, because if I said any more, something bad would happen to my parents.' Later on they also remembered many events which had seemed irrelevant, but which it became clear afterwards were vital evidence. A year later they came forward with the whole story in an attempt to get the case reopened. This was not granted, but it did persuade the authorities that a period of time should be left between taking evidence and bringing a prosecution. The period was set at three months. Its purpose was to allow time for more complete reports to be taken from the women and to prevent them from retracting their statements through fear. The women also needed time to consider the consequences of making a statement and the resulting court case.

The next contribution to Dutch law was made by an illegal South American immigrant, who was explicitly not a victim of traffic in women. She went public with her story, calling herself by the name Teresa. 'I came to the Netherlands of my own accord to make some money. I was indebted to nobody and I could work on my own terms. However, my window looked over houses on the other side of the street. There I saw a girl being beaten up and dragged out by the hair. Next I noticed that the other women were not free to leave the building and they were continuously watched by some men. At last I could not stand it any more and discussed it with a friend. She advised me against it, but eventually I went to the police to warn them. That was a mistake, they put me in prison as an illegal immigrant.'[6] She was later released and sued the state successfully for damages.

Through her perseverance illegal immigrants who are not victims but witnesses can also stay legally in the Netherlands while they are needed for a trial.

Attitudes to women who testify

A now classic argument which defence counsel use is that women go to the police and make statements only to obtain this legal status, and that it is possible for a woman to present a cock and bull story for this purpose. One or two women have tried, but they were soon found out. Their traffickers forced them to make false statements at the police station and made them work again afterwards. However, as a rule it is extremely difficult to sustain a false statement without making mistakes. The police need evidence and any untruths are likely to be found out.

The Rotterdam foreigners' police spokesman said, 'Why should a woman do that? She alienates herself from her associates. Next she notices that those who were not so courageous continue to work to line their own pockets.' The temporary permit of residence is not desirable because it only postpones expulsion. It is easier to get a residence permit by marrying a Dutch national than go through the martyrdom of denunciation. In fact, women with legal status also filed complaints, as did women who wanted to be returned home voluntarily. In 1993, 28 of STV's 88 clients wanted

to go home and in 1992 the figures were 17 out of 70.[7] STV
hardly ever hears from women who return to their own countries,
presumably because they want to forget the past. In one case a
rogatory commission was sent after them, which proved embar-
rassing. A large delegation of police and public prosecutors arrived
in a village in Indonesia, making it public knowledge that a girl
was being sought by the police, even if only as a witness. From
that day on, she did not dare to leave the house. At least two other
women are known to have been pursued by traffickers in their
own countries.

Reprisals and after-effects

One Yugoslavian client of STV was shot in the street in the Netherlands. The police didn't relate her death to the fact that she had
denounced traffickers, but a question mark remains. Another
trafficked girl was persecuted in Poland by her traffickers. When
her brother tried to protect her, his arm was broken.

While they are in the Netherlands they are entitled to social
security, but women who have conditional residence permits are
not entitled to work permits. They resent living on social security
and want to earn their living: which is, after all, why most of them
came in the first place. They know there is one job for which the
bosses never ask to see a permit: prostitution. Some women go
back on the game, including those who were forced on to it
before. With their previous experience they have developed the
skills necessary for prostitution, such as the dissociation of emotion
and sexuality. Besides, the only people they know live in this
subculture.

Some women are afraid they have contracted AIDS; up till now,
however, only one client of STV has died of AIDS. One trafficked
woman who didn't go to STV for help also became a victim of the
disease. Health workers report that the number of cases of AIDS
among male and female migrants is increasing slightly. It is
unknown whether they were infected by their partner, in prostitution or way back in their homeland. At least five of STV's clients
were forced to have abortions. Women who have abortions voluntarily are not counted as victims of sexual violence.

Only a minority of the women go back to prostitution; most
want to make a clean break. They are afraid of the traffickers and
their associates, which is why they have to stay in shelters whose

addresses are not revealed. But because of these security measures they feel isolated. Occasionally they can stay as guests with a family or in a convent. Three Russian women lived with a Dutch nun. They had the surprise of their lives when they saw the sister driving a car and whistling while doing repairs around the house. 'We'll never forget the emancipated sister,' they said gratefully on leaving. The staff of the shelters do everything to help the women cope with their emotional problems.[8] Women trafficked on a small scale for marriage are often in an especially bad emotional state. Most suffer from psychosomatic disorders. Most trafficked women are homesick and confused; some have lost their homes and jobs. They miss their children, whom they have left in the care of a grandmother or other relatives. Some women become pregnant after rape or 'an accident with a customer'. One of these children, whom I met, is already four years old. He asked, 'Where is my father?' When his mother didn't answer, he grabbed his toy telephone and fantasized a conversation with his unknown father.

Some victims are still children themselves. STV's records seem to show that younger and younger women are applying for help. In 1992 the women were on average 26 years old; in 1993 they were 23. But older women are also being trafficked: the youngest was 13, the oldest 51. Minors are generally sent back to their parents, who have sometimes reported them missing.

The police

A group of 15 policemen from several divisions were assembled for a briefing on a well-prepared raid. Many translators had spent hours in a laboratory listening to the tapped phone calls of a gang. The timing of the raid had been carefully planned so that the few customers present could be instructed to sneak out secretly. The police chief explained the lie of the land and read out the anonymous letter from a client which had been the starting point of the action. The man had been shocked by the conditions in which the women had to work.

From the outside the brothel looked luxurious and picturesquely situated, but appearances were deceptive. Only the hall where punters were welcomed looked attractive, with its red velvet settee. The working rooms were a mess: the beds were too high and a price list written in felt-tipped pen on cardboard was the only decoration.

In the living room there were cups of half-drunk coffee; newly lit cigarettes had been quickly stubbed out; a piece of bread was going stale: all signs of a hasty departure. A desk drawer had been forced open by one of the women looking for her passport.

Afterwards it turned out that three victims were among the illegal women rounded up. During the raid they were pacing up and down, pretending to be handcuffed. They tried to communicate to the police that they felt like prisoners.[9] News of raids has a way of leaking out, deliberately or by accident, for example by eavesdropping on police scanners. The women reported that they had had to hide shortly before the police arrived because the boss had been warned beforehand.

To achieve more effective policing of traffic in women, in 1988 the Dutch Department of Justice issued policy directives. They state that assumed victims of traffic should not be expelled but referred to support organizations. One directive directs the police to maintain links with prostitution to detect traffic.

The police forces which apply this directive are aware of its inherent dangers. Officers Bennink and De Winter of the Rotterdam police: 'When we visit these houses we cannot ignore the manager. When a girl sees us speaking to him, she may think that we are corrupt. That's how the rumours start that we take bribes and we want a free go. We know the bosses use this argument against us.' It is a classic trick of traffickers to misinform women that they are in league with the police. 'You might stop the gossiping by avoiding sex clubs altogether. But then the managers can do what they please, without us knowing anything.' Women believe their bosses and assume the police are corrupt, because they often are in their home countries. Research has pointed out there are some incidents of police corruption, but it is not widespread in the Netherlands.[10]

Women don't always understand police tactics: they are surprised when prostitutes are not arrested, which reinforces their belief that the police turn a blind eye. Often they don't know that prostitution is not illegal in the Netherlands. It takes time for them to understand that they haven't been arrested for prostitution but because they are illegal immigrants. Most of these women go to great lengths to avoid the police, but others can't wait for the police to raid the clubs or brothels. 'At last, it was about time,' one woman said during a raid.

Recently the Dutch policy directives have been re-evaluated.[11] The results were shocking. Not all police forces put the directives into practice, nor did they tackle the problems in a uniform manner. Though the law condemns all trafficking of prostitutes, some policemen are concerned only with women who definitely didn't know they were entering prostitution. The directive that supposed victims of traffic must not be deported immediately is not always heeded. Some police forces are not prepared to spend time and money on combating traffic, which is why the Rotterdam police, who were pioneers in tackling traffic in women, have backed out of prostitution control and stopped investigating traffic altogether.

Reporting by people other than the police

'Look, right now I have many Thai girls in the waiting room here at the STD [sexually transmitted diseases] clinic waiting for a health check-up,' a doctor said when I called him at a busy time. Angrily he continued, 'From their bodies I can tell these girls are only 13. But they have papers, probably false, stating that they are over 18. What can I do? I have my professional code of secrecy and besides, I have been threatened with a knife before.' He is one of the few doctors in close contact with these women.

Although it is the role of the police to investigate and uncover trafficking in women, other professionals are also involved. Once or twice doctors have warned STV when they suspect a woman has been trafficked. In quite a few cases women stop a passer-by, who takes them to a social worker or to the police. Lawyers, fellow prostitutes and social workers also find victims. In 1993 ten clients were brought to STV by private individuals, whereas in 1992 that happened only once.[12] In 1992, 26 of the 70 women who contacted STV had been sent by the police, and in 1993 the number had risen to 57 out of a total of 88.[13] Sometimes brothel-keepers or punters put the women in contact with support organizations. Punters can play an important role, but it is not easy to mobilize them.

Men who use prostitutes can't easily find out whether they have been trafficked or not: the women don't always confide in them. Besides, the women know they have to keep smiling to attract the punters. Gerrit, who visits prostitutes regularly, said, 'In The Hague I once had a newcomer to the job. When I was inside people were shouting instructions to the girl through the window, so I understood, though I don't speak Spanish. I left straight away, because I didn't want any trouble. On another occasion I was with a naïve girl who clearly hated the job. I paid her and left without touching her. By the way, you shouldn't overdo it. Most women work voluntarily. In Amsterdam I have never come across a window prostitute who was trafficked.' Like Gerrit, most punters don't want a woman who has been forced on to the game. Sometimes they pluck up their courage and help a girl who has been trafficked to get away.

Frequenters of night clubs have less trouble in coming out than clients of window prostitutes because they can say they were 'just having a beer in a club'. Sometimes these knights in shining armour press the women to go to the police. So one Thai woman arrived with her client at the police station. This man noisily demanded that the police raid the club, if necessary with violence. He would not allow her to speak to the police in private. An elderly detective put him in his place: 'You are angered by the infringement of her human dignity, but now you should respect her too. She can very well speak for herself.' Another woman left her rescuer, fearing that he would take the law in his own hands. He said to her, 'I am no good myself. I have been convicted for violent assault. I know I can handle these people more effectively than the police.'

Quite a few women start a relationship with their clients because they are the only outsiders they know. Besides, it offers an alternative to the temporary residence permit. In some cases marriage results. Some of these marriages work, others don't. Most of the romances come to an untimely end. Couples usually clash over the issue of sending money to the woman's family in her home country. One relationship broke up when the groom was convicted before the marriage could take place. At least two of STV's clients were 'saved' by Dutch punters who then employed them in their own brothels.

Unfortunately STV can only help women who are considering pressing charges or are in the process of doing so, and so have temporary legal status. Those who don't dare to press charges have to remain hidden. Social services are not available for them.

The current legal situation

Following discussions the laws against trafficking in women have been amended. Sex-club owners or traffickers can be taken to court if they use force or violence. There are now several grounds on which a woman can be defined as having been trafficked, including women brought into prostitution under false pretences. The majority of STV's clients didn't know they were going to become prostitutes.[14] Other women who knew they were going to work as prostitutes became victims of traffic when they were misled about their working conditions. They never agreed to hand over their earnings or their documents. They were not bound in their contracts to endure being locked up, violence or threats. The law states that it is illegal for women to be made dependent on the services of traffickers; the official wording is bringing a person into prostitution by 'force or violence or by abusing one's ascendancy derived from actual relations'. Moreover it is forbidden to take women across national borders for the sole purpose of prostituting them. Last but not least, the new law is not gender specific, but also recognizes the traffic in boys and men.[15]

Managers of sex houses

'Like me, many women were forced into prostitution. I get very angry when I hear that they only fuss about foreign women,' a Dutch ex-prostitute said. She had been terrorized and kept prisoner for a considerable length of time by a pimp. She was right to consider herself a victim, but she was a victim of pimping not trafficking. Under the new Dutch law, transporting women across national borders is a vital characteristic of traffic.

Trafficking doesn't only occur in major cities with red light districts. Trafficked women can also be found in small villages in the Netherlands and elsewhere. Nowadays traffickers prefer rural areas where the police are less alert. Until recently in the Netherlands most trafficked women worked in clubs, where 80 per cent of the prostitution takes place, and behind the windows. Nowadays they are working as escorts and even on the streets. Street-corner workers report that eastern European women come in pairs and some are known to have been sent by criminal organizations. Formerly only small-time criminals, mostly drug addicts, forced their girlfriends to work in kerb-crawling areas. A minority of trafficked women, especially Moroccan and Chinese, work in private houses.

Not all traffickers are brothel-keepers and not all brothel-keepers are traffickers. Nowadays brothel-owners who knowingly hire trafficked girls are considered accomplices. In 1992 Klein Beekman of Verenjin Exploitanten Relaxhuizen (VER), the Dutch Association of Relaxhouses (a euphemism for sex clubs) stated that one-third of the owners of the 3,000 houses of prostitution in the

Netherlands were involved in criminal activities. By 1994 he was not so sure of the figure. He said, 'We want to outnumber the bad operators. We have already refused a company which was known to deal in arms, minors and drugs.' He agreed that traffic is a serious problem which damages the respectable image the association needs to support its claim to be legalized. 'Only the genuine sex-club owners join us, if only to safeguard their investments.'

5 Thailand to Europe: a one-way ticket

In the district of Korat in Thailand there is a small village where most of the young women have left for Germany. The teacher's sister recruited them to be prostitutes in Berlin. To pay for their travel several incurred enormous debts. The teacher's sister had to stop trafficking because she was under suspicion, but another sibling carried on the family business. Twenty women went to Berlin, encouraged by their families to take jobs abroad. Some parents went so far as to persuade them to divorce their Thai husbands in order to marry a German; one woman had paid 5,000 marks for this. The women who returned home had found there was no way they could make a living. One of them had contracted AIDS.[1]

These women emigrated according to the one-step pattern, that is directly from the rural areas to their foreign destination. Women who do this usually have no experience of being on the game and have very high expectations of life abroad.[2] Women who move from the country to the big cities and then go abroad through agencies or as tourists are following what is called the two-step pattern.

Not until 1985 did the Thai government take measures to repress trafficking. The authorities stated that women who applied for a passport who were under 36, had little money and were travelling alone, had to be thoroughly screened. However, this only criminalized women who wanted to travel independently. To avoid being caught travelling alone, they had to use dubious middlemen.

More effective action has been taken by non-governmental organizations such as the Women's Information Centre and EMPOWER (Education Means Protection of Women Engaged in Recreation). EMPOWER wants to improve working conditions for Thai prostitutes, which are generally bad because the bosses have a great deal of power over them. Most women have to pay commission to the bar owner just to be in his bar and they are fined if they are late. EMPOWER says, 'It is very difficult for a Thai woman to become the owner of a bar. The most they can hope for is to become a "mamasan", a supervisor of girls.' Exploitation of prostitutes became a worldwide issue when a brothel at Phuket caught fire in 1984. The women, some of whom were in chains, could not escape and were burned alive. The brothel-owner, Mr Koleng, was later sentenced to life imprisonment; his wife received a three-year sentence as an accomplice.

Another problem is police corruption: for every girl working in a bar, the owner has to pay a fee to the police. Thai women's groups are discussing the legalization of prostitution to give women some control and also to limit police corruption. Prostitution was banned in Thailand in 1960.

Thailand does not only export prostitutes: it is also becoming a target country for girls from Burma and China; 20,000 Burmese women and girls work in Thai brothels.[3] Even the Thai police are reputed to traffic in Burmese girls.[4] Because of their geographical and political isolation Burmese women are supposed to be free from AIDS.[5] There are two routes out of China to northern Thailand via Burma. One is a small road in southern Xichuanpanna passable only by motorcycles and tractors. This route takes three days. The other way is to cross the mountain forests on foot to northern Xichuanpanna, a 20-day walk. Most Burmese women are recruited by Thai middlemen, who hand them over to Burmese men, with whom they travel to the Thai border. At the border they are collected by another Thai group, which takes them to Bangkok and to the south, where they entertain Malaysian tourists. In Thailand the meeting point for smuggled women is Mae Sai, the northernmost district, which is separated from Burma by a small river. The lorry drivers pay off the Burmese officials at the checkpoint. As a result of the civil war in Burma, which has been fought now for 45 years, many civilians have fled to refugee camps near the Thai border. The women and girls in these camps are easy prey for traffickers.

There are also Vietnamese women working in Thai brothels. Some of them were hijacked by Thai pirates when they were fleeing their countries in boats.[6] Even Colombian women have been forced into prostitution in Thailand. Colombian traffickers have joined up with Thai traffickers for this purpose.[7]

The evidence that an increasing number of Thai women were being trafficked to western Europe became clear from the 1970s onwards. In their struggles to provide for themselves and their families they had sought help from acquaintances, who had put them in touch with traffickers. They were promised jobs or marriage once they had paid large sums in commission and for what turned out to be either non-existent or forged documents. They were then flown to the easiest European points of entry – Denmark or the Czech Republic – and smuggled across the borders into, for example, Germany or the Netherlands. Because they did not have work permits and because they 'owed' large sums to the traffickers, they were powerless, although sometimes they managed to get away.

'Surely this is not a restaurant?'

In January 1991 in the northern Dutch town of Den Helder three Thai girls made a remarkable escape. One, named Tip, jumped out of a window on to the top of a police car in which her friends Tina and Da were already safe. They also had jumped from the window of the sex club where they had been locked up.

Soon afterwards the women made statements. Tip and Da decided to return to Thailand as soon as their evidence had been heard by the examining magistrate. Tina stayed on in the Netherlands until the trial. I spoke to Da and Tip before they left for Bangkok and Tina gave me further details later. Their stories, which ended so spectacularly, started with the promise of well-paid jobs in Europe.

For Tip and Da it began with the Thai woman W., who recruited three of the six women who were taken to Den Helder. Tip met W. through a caretaker in a school where her aunt was a teacher. 'The caretaker asked me whether I would like a job in the Netherlands. Of course I said yes and later he gave me W.'s name. I went to see her and she promised me I could work for an excellent salary as a waitress in a restaurant. At the time I didn't know her well, but I was impressed by her luxurious apartment. That's why I believed her instantly. I knew she had lived in the Netherlands, but she never told me she had worked as a prostitute. She only mentioned that I needed a passport and tickets. Before everything was arranged I had to visit W. several times. In the meantime I had to find the money to pay her commission for providing me with the travel documents. She also claimed she had to order suitable working clothes for me. They turned out to be a bundle of cheap second-hand rags.'

Tip did not realize that she would be working as a prostitute. She only knew that she had to drink with clients. 'I thought that was normal. When I worked in a restaurant in Thailand, I also had drinks with customers, but I never had to sleep with them.'

Da, Tip's partner in misfortune, was also recruited by W. But W. had unceremoniously told her beforehand that she would be a prostitute. Da was already waitressing in a bar where she sometimes slept with clients. 'That was different. I spoke the language and I was my own boss,' she said. 'A few times W. dropped in at the bar where I worked. On one occasion she told me she had made a fortune in the Netherlands. At first I didn't believe her. I thought she was bragging. To win me over she invited me to her house. I changed my mind when I saw how she lived.'

Da was taken in by W.'s wealth. 'W. told me I would get a certain percentage of what clients paid the club. I was going to make ten dollars just for drinking a bottle of champagne.' This is the regular fee for hostess work, but Da was to earn nothing. W. didn't tell her that she would only start to earn after she had paid off her debts.

Before leaving Thailand, Da thought she only owed W. the commission. When W. kept on asking for more money, Da became suspicious. 'First W. asked me for 5,000 baht, which I had to borrow from a neighbour. That was not enough. I had to pay up more and more, but W. never gave me notice that I could set out for Europe. However, I could not back out because I would lose the money I had already paid. Eventually I went.'

There are many procuresses like W. in Thailand. Indeed her own story is a sad one. On her first trip to Europe she found herself in the hands of traffickers. Instead of pressing charges, she decided to co-operate with them; unfortunately this didn't help her. On her return to the Netherlands they locked her up until she had paid her debts.

Tina, the third girl who told me her story, was not recruited by W., but by a girl called Jacky. 'In a bar she introduced me to Jan, the owner of the sex club where I could work in the near future. Jacky said to him, pointing at me, "Nice girl, you want?"' Tina had to pay Jacky a large sum for this small service.

Some weeks later Tina was put on a plane to Prague with Da, Tip and three other girls. Da and Tip had a photograph of Jan, whom Tina had met already in the bar. He was waiting for them at the airport and they were glad someone had turned up to collect them.

They set off for the Netherlands in two cars. Tina said, 'Jan drove and somebody else read the map. For some hours nothing happened. We just talked and slept till the car stopped in the middle of nowhere. "Get out," Jan said. "You have to walk the next bit."'

The six women, shivering in their flimsy summer clothes and on high heels, had to walk for a few hours to cross the German border on foot. They had to be smuggled in because they didn't have visas for Germany or the Netherlands. As they walked it dawned on them that they were now illegal immigrants, but they felt it was too late to turn back. On the other side of the border they continued their journey by car. Tina and Da found out that the two recruiters, Jacky and W., worked for the same sex clubs.

Once in the Netherlands the girls discovered that Jan, who in Thailand had been described as the big boss, was in reality small fry. He worked for someone else. Tina said, 'Jan was a bit of a buffoon. Sometimes he was even nice. I didn't want to argue with him all the time.' Jan was not very clever and didn't make much from trafficking in women, in fact it caused his bankruptcy. According to Tina, he was taken advantage of by his boss, Jacques, who was well known to the Dutch police. Jacques had threatened Tina. 'That monster told me, I could kill you and nobody will find out. Nobody knows you are here.' He owned several sex clubs, some of them in Thailand. Jan had recently bought one of Jacques' clubs and wanted to staff it with the recently imported Thai women. He was foolish enough to sign the contract of purchase just after the police had raided the club, which gave the police solid evidence against him.

When they reached Den Helder the women were made to sign a paper stating they were indebted to Jan and Jacques for their fare and for the detour via the Czech Republic. They also had to pay for their accommodation in the sex club. Jan's Thai wife (who had been put to work as a prostitute) acted as translator, but didn't translate literally. She made out that she was reading them a normal employment contract, but the women later discovered that what they had signed was a confession of debt. The contract stipulated they would not receive any money until they had paid off their debts. After that their salary would be half what an independent prostitute earns. It also obliged them to provide any service a punter might ask for. They were even forbidden to make friends. They signed reluctantly in order to start paying off their debts. To prevent them from running away, they were made to hand over their passports immediately. Finally they were told they had to hide in a secret room reached by a connecting door in the event of a raid.

'Surely this is not a restaurant?' Tip remarked when she walked into the recently painted sex club for the first time. Unlike Tina and Da, she had not known that she was expected to work as a prostitute. She was met with derisive laughter. Jan had hammered it into her that she had to pay her debts; and made it clear that the only way to do this was by having sex with the clients. Tip told me, 'The first day I tried to limit myself to drinking champagne with customers. But the men didn't want to leave it at that and took me upstairs. Then I always told them they were my first client. "Me no work in business," I said. Sometimes they took pity on me – after all, I look younger than my age, so nobody caught me lying. One of the punters realized he had a daughter of my assumed age at home, who was sleeping in her own bed. He dashed out of the room. The bosses didn't mind as long as the clients paid up.'

As Tip spoke hardly any English, Tina negotiated with the clients for her. In broken English, she would say, 'Pay 100 guilders half a hour, 200 guilders one o'clock,' Tip added laughing.

Tip had more difficulty working with the clients than her friends, who had experience on the game and who had at least learned to protect themselves against AIDS. However, here they were not always allowed to use condoms, especially not with clients who were acquaintances of the managers.

One of the six women had a very special client, a Scottish sailor who came to the club and bought her for £1,000. Soon afterwards he took pity on her and sent her back to Thailand, from where she wrote to the girls she had left behind.

As well as not receiving a penny, the women were locked up throughout their stay in Den Helder. Once or twice they were allowed outside, accompanied by Jan. When the last client had gone, Jan would lock the club up and leave the women on their own. None of the telephones worked. The women were also afraid of fire because there was no emergency exit.

Tina decided to put an end to this. She had not told Jan that she had the telephone number of a Thai girl in Rotterdam. She smashed one of the windows, climbed out and went to look for a phone booth. She managed to phone her friend, who immediately called the Rotterdam police, who in turn contacted their colleagues in Den Helder. Events moved quickly. Though the other girls were frightened, they plucked up their courage and jumped out of the window which Tina had broken. Tip was the last to escape.

The Rotterdam policeman who took part in the release of the girls, Bert Bennink, said, 'I didn't want to be a knight in shining armour, but I thought it inhuman just to write a report and leave it at that. Fortunately I had good contacts with colleagues in the north.' After the police car had left, Jan arrived to find his brothel empty. To his surprise he learned the police, who had entered the building, had also taken his wife, mistaking her for a victim. She was put with the victims, who understandably became very taciturn in her presence. Jan went to the police to give himself up.

To date no one has been convicted because obtaining evidence was difficult. Tina gave seemingly conflicting evidence to the examining magistrate. He had asked her to answer his questions as far as possible with a simple yes or no, which she did; so when he asked whether the door of the sex club was locked from the inside, she said yes. Next the magistrate wanted to know if she had a key. Tina again said, 'Yes.' She assumed that she was not allowed to say that Jan locked the door from the outside with a second key.

The examining magistrate then asked, 'Could you leave the room?', to which Tina replied, 'No.' The examining magistrate could only conclude he had contradictory statements on his hands.

Most of the women involved in this case are now back in Thailand. Just before leaving Tip was plagued by feelings of guilt. 'I am still trying to convince myself it was not my fault. At first I thought it all happened to me as a punishment for wanting to be rich.' Like many Thai girls she believed in the Buddhist concept of karma: that future events are the result of one's actions in the past.

The route through Prague is relatively new. Bert Bennink, the Rotterdam policeman, said, 'Nowadays Thai people need a visa for most European countries, but not for the Czech Republic. And *vroom*, the women are driven by car to the Netherlands, before you can say Jack Robinson.' Nowadays many women from South America also travel via Prague. Other Thai girls arriving by plane come via Copenhagen because they don't need a visa for Denmark.

Other cases from Thailand

The story of Tip, Da and Tina is one of small-scale trafficking in women: sex-club owners scouring Bangkok or other Third World cities for women they can con. Jan's method was typical of trafficking in the 1970s and the early 1980s. Like Jan, many sex-club owners became romantically involved with the women they hired to work in Europe. Much small-scale trafficking is a direct result of tourism.

Many Thai women who married after 'falling in love' with a tourist are now working as prostitutes. The husbands claim their salaries or social security money are not enough to support their wives and their families in Thailand. One husband told me, 'She considers herself forced, not by people, but by circumstance. Her family thinks luxury grows on trees. I hope my daughters will never find out where she is working. I am always nervous when she is at work. I am particularly worried about the neighbours, who eventually might put two and two together.'

Two large-scale court cases involving Thai women came before the Dutch courts in 1988. One concerned three Dutchmen who had trafficked three Thai women. This case was controversial because a policeman claimed the women could not have been trafficked since he had seen them laughing. Later on he admitted that trafficked women don't necessarily have to cry all the time. In reality they are not allowed to cry because they might put off the customers. In a second case three brothers had recruited five women through a Thai middleman. The brothers started a fight with the broker because the women he had procured for them were too old. They had wanted girls of 15.

In 1990 a case came to court in the Dutch-German border region. Only one victim testified against the gang. Clutching the Buddha pendant on her neck, she said, 'I am going to make talk.' She was terrified because one of the traffickers had smashed up the house of the client who released her. Because there were no other witnesses the traffickers left the court free men, while the victim and her companion had to depart under police protection. Four years later one of the gang was still operating. Some foreign women he employed complained of exploitation but didn't press charges. He was seen recently on television boasting that he had about 60 girls working for him in several countries.

Another Thai woman played a major role in a bigger case in 1990. Seven Thai women were recruited and promised jobs as domestic helpers. Several traffickers were involved, some of whom were sex-club owners. The police were alerted when one of the traffickers unwittingly came to the police station to register his girlfriend as a prostitute. She turned out to be a former victim who had chosen to work with the traffickers, as W. had.

The recruiters were helped in Thailand by a civil servant who provided women with the forged birth certificates they needed to marry. The victims were paid £2 a day and were married off to strangers to give them legal status. When they arrived they were raped to break their resistance and then made to work in the Amsterdam red light district. They dared not and could not run away. One girl became troublesome and the traffickers considered dumping her on a German autobahn. The gang later threatened the girls and one of the policemen handling the case.

In 1990 a third case failed. It concerned a sex-club owner who went to Thailand pretending to be a wholesale fashion importer and enticed women to work for him in the Netherlands. The police were alerted by neighbours, who complained of the public nuisance in the village. They were also tipped off by the Thai community. When the police raided the club, bystanders who didn't live in the neighbourhood tried to prevent what they thought was police harassment of the girls, believing that in a country like the Netherlands prostitution should be tolerated. It was all to no avail. The Thai girls had disappeared because the owner had been warned about the raid.[8]

One of the most recent cases involving Thai women occurred in April 1993. The police found five Thai women and a Russian in an empty apartment, where they had been abandoned without food. The traffickers had vanished because they had heard rumours that they were to be raided. The boys had met one of the women when they were on holiday in Thailand and returned later to invite her and her friends to the Netherlands. One of the women asked them to find her a job in Dutch prostitution, which they agreed to arrange. Her friends then followed suit and the women travelled to the Netherlands via Denmark. The recruiters had organized a bogus marriage for one of the women. Luckily for her, the husband-to-be liked her and said he would marry her for free. The marriage hadn't taken place by the time the police intervened. 'Just whistle and you have a Boeing full of Thai girls,' one of the boys said in his defence. 'It all happened in a friendly atmosphere. We only wanted to help the girls.'

The judge at their trial said, 'The girl did in fact want to work as a prostitute but she didn't bargain with being tied by a debt of 200,000 guilders.' The women didn't know that they would be illegal immigrants. Before leaving Thailand, the girl had agreed to pay for the necessary papers, but the amount she owed had soared overnight.

'Why was the sum of money so ridiculously high?' the judge asked the boys. 'Charge 1,000 or 2,000, what's the difference?' one replied casually. The boys had not even given the women their small share of the deal.

They had threatened the family of one of the women and had told the girls that they had guns. 'I'm the kind of guy who likes to flash a firearm,' one boy said coolly.

The women regarded the boy who acted as their chauffeur as their protector because he was less violent than his friends. Every day the girls had to hand him their earnings in an envelope from which he helped himself to his own share. He was convicted of being an accomplice. In court he admitted that he had wanted set up in business on his own. A Russian girl, whom he had nicknamed Gorbachev, already worked for him. He had not recruited her himself, but had taken her over. 'I took pity on the Russian girl. That's why I tried to help her.'

The chauffeur said he preferred trafficking in women to drugs because he thought it was easier. The other two boys were already drug traffickers and had started trading in women to remedy a temporary shortage of money – the trafficking of drugs is dangerous because the goods have to be bought and sold fast. Paying with cash is the only way to do this; with any other method the risk of being caught is too great.

The three boys hadn't realized that trafficking in women was so complicated. They had had to deal with a local pimp who had threatened to 'steal' one of the girls: it was the resulting car chase which had caught the police's attention. All three were convicted.

The declining Thai market

The numbers of Thai women coming to Europe lessened after the arrival of women from eastern Europe and the traffic between Thailand and Japan increased. 'Nowadays Thai women need a visa for Germany. Their transportation to Japan, Taiwan and Hong Kong is much cheaper. Most women go in groups to Japan by bus and pay much money for their visa and passports. They don't go independently. They always have to know someone who arranges the necessary papers,' two prostitutes from EMPOWER said, when visiting the Netherlands.

The threat of AIDS is one of the reasons why sex tourism from Europe to Thailand has dwindled. Through street theatre, the women of EMPOWER persuade customers in the bars in Thai seaside resorts to use condoms. This is necessary because the number of AIDS victims has increased dramatically in Thailand. Pollution of the beaches has also played its part in decreasing the number of sex tourists to the country. Thailand is now trying to restore the seaside as a place for family outings.[9]

6 Colombian gangs: they see everything

'It was a scandal. You should have seen me, lying there delivering my baby without help. I had cut the umbilical cord by myself. Then the police arrived and took me and my baby to the hospital.' Maria from Colombia was still upset when she recalled the birth of her baby several years later.

It all started because Maria badly needed a steady job. 'In Colombia I met a girl at a party, who knew a very rich woman. My friend invited me to go with her to this woman's house. I was curious, so I went along. The lady lived in a big house and of course I wanted to know how she had paid for it. She told me she had earned it all as a babysitter abroad. I said I wished I could go to Europe. To my surprise she assured me that it could easily be arranged. A friend of hers would send me a ticket as soon as I had saved enough money to pay the expenses.'

It took Maria a year to save the necessary amount for the broker, a woman who had left for Greece in the meantime. Every now and then the broker would write to Maria to keep her informed. At last Maria heard from Greece that a Dutchman wanted her as a domestic worker. The broker promised to take care of everything from Greece. After a few weeks Maria received her ticket. 'My mother implored me not to go. She thought it was all so dubious. But I turned a deaf ear because I had gone to so much trouble already. Besides, I had nothing at all in Colombia.' Maria did not know that she could not get a normal job on the tourist visa she had been given. She arrived at Schiphol airport in Amsterdam in good spirits. She began to realize that something was wrong when the immigration officers asked her to show them that she had the necessary money for her stay. When she couldn't she was immediately sent to the airport police.

Nowadays traffickers avoid this problem by lending the women so-called showmoney, which has to be returned as soon as they have passed through immigration control. Maria, however, only had an air ticket and the telephone number of her future employer. In the office of the airport police a further surprise was in store. 'There were more Colombian women with a note with my employer's telephone number scribbled on it. I had seen these women on the plane, but I hadn't talked to them. At last the police let me call my future boss. A Dutchman answered the phone and wanted to speak to all of us. "Stay there tonight. Tomorrow you will all be picked up," he told us.'

The next day the employer arrived and paid £900 guarantee for Maria. The man, who was a complete stranger to her, told the police bluntly that he had lived with her in Colombia. Apparently he had lived there years before and spoke the language. Later the other 'Colombianas' were picked up by different men.

It was some weeks before Maria learned their fate. 'I met one of them in the sex club where I had to make money for him. The guys who came to meet them were probably associates of my so-called employer. I don't really know; at the time I had other things on my mind.' They might also have been in touch with the woman in Greece who had procured Maria for her employer. There were other Colombian women who lived with him. On the very first day the man confiscated her passport and told her that she would only get it back when she had paid him back the guarantee. Maria began to doubt his intentions, but thought he must return her passport. She only had to brace herself for a few months of hard work.

On the very first night he forced Maria to sleep with him. 'Of course I didn't have the pill with me since I never expected to have intercourse. Next he told me he wanted to live with me. I said, "What the hell do you mean? I don't even know you. I came here as a cleaning lady and nothing else." "No señora, tomorrow you are going to work in a bar," he said.' By now Maria knew that she was trapped.

The bar the Dutchman sent Maria to was a sex club where several Colombian women worked, including some of the women who lived in Maria's employer's house. She felt them watching her. Maria said later, 'What could I do? I had no money and no passport. Besides, I was afraid of this man.'

After a few months Maria realized to her dismay that she was becoming heavier and heavier. 'I was hardly up to my work, but

I didn't want to admit that I had become pregnant as a result of the rape. But the other girls noticed my physical changes and warned me, "You look like you could do with a doctor." That started me thinking.'

Maria had no health insurance and could not pay for the doctor herself. She still had to give all the money she earned to the Dutchman. 'I was afraid he might kill me if he found out that because of my pregnancy I couldn't work any longer. Then I heard that you could rent a prostitution window in The Hague with no questions asked about papers and legal status. My tourist visa had expired long since, so I went to The Hague secretly. I didn't want the other Colombians who worked in the club to know where I was going. I thought they were all in league with my employer. Going to The Hague was a big step, since he had taken not just my money but my clothes as well, to stop me running away.

'I managed to get a room where I could hide. I took enough customers to be able to pay the rent. I had to, because under no circumstances did I want to go back to that man. I slept in the room where I worked and never went out on the streets. Once in a while the other girls would bring me some food. They thought I was crazy. They tried to be friends with me, but I turned my back on them because I was afraid they might contact the man to tell him where I was.

'In The Hague I still didn't dare see a doctor. Yet I wanted to because I was afraid working with clients might hurt my baby. Then I caught an infection which made me very ill. I was afraid to go to hospital since I could not pay the bill and I thought they would throw me in jail. I decided to deliver the baby all by myself. In the meantime I tried to distract my mind by reading the magazines the other girls gave me. I was afraid too much worrying would harm the baby.'

Maria managed to satisfy most of her customers by giving them massage, but in her seventh month she had a client who wanted more. When Maria refused he became so angry that he kicked her in the belly. At that moment contractions started. The customer bolted out of the room because he didn't want any trouble. A passing colleague saw that Maria was in labour and couldn't believe her eyes. Maria said, 'Though I begged her not to, she went out to call the police. She didn't want to leave me like that. The police came to take me to the hospital. I felt ashamed because I had nothing, no nightgown, no baby clothes, nothing. Several people came to my bedside, but I refused to speak to anyone.

Everybody was quite nice and helpful but I was terrible,' she said, still embarrassed after all these years. 'But now everything has changed.'

Indeed it has. The child is healthy and well. Maria is married to a Dutchman and now really works as a cleaner. After her baby was born she went to the police, but there was insufficient evidence to convict the man who trapped her. The police did nothing about the woman in Greece. Not until a few years later were they alerted to the 'Greek connection' (see chapter 8).

Manuel

Marcia was one of many Colombian prostitutes working in Europe. In Colombia she was a so-called *prostituta reservada* with a choice of customers, especially tourists. These women are relatively independent and work without pimps.[1] Then Marcia met a man we will call 'Manuel', who cajoled her into leaving the country with him. Later she and four women from the Dominican Republic found themselves in the Netherlands being exploited in Dutch prostitution.

Marcia told me, 'In Colombia there are no pimps as there are here. Only my family lived off my money. Prostitution in Colombia is much better than here: there is a doctor, you are paid during holidays and you are tipped well when you drink with customers or wait on their tables. I am so sorry I left all that behind for just an illusion.'

Marcia had met Manuel in a discothèque in Bogotá. As he had with his other victims, he promised to marry her, which Marcia thought would give her the opportunity to make a fortune in Dutch prostitution. He took her to Belgium, where at the time visa regulations for Colombians were less strict than in the Netherlands. From there she was taken to the Netherlands, where, much to her surprise, she became an illegal immigrant. She said, 'That was not agreed on. He said he would give me money to buy myself a forged passport in Spain. I said no, I didn't want to work to pay for plastic surgery to get my face adjusted to the one on the passport. You can change my name but not my face. When he told me I had to hand him all my money, I didn't understand what he meant. He can't do that, I thought.'

At the house of the customer with whom Marcia was living when I met her, I also talked to Ana, her partner in misfortune. The two women had become close friends when they had to work in the same brothel for Manuel. While Marcia did Ana's hair, they both spoke at the tops of their voices about the reign of terror Manuel had exercised over them. For instance, he told them they would be killed if they got too fat: they were so afraid that they hardly ate at all. There was no time to take a rest, and Ana was locked up and beaten several times. She didn't even know what city she was working in. 'You know, it was in the town where there was a tobacconist,' she said helpfully. At intervals the women forgot their hairdressing activities to act out their conversations with Manuel and his many accomplices.

In the meantime Marcia took pictures of Ana and me. Like many other amateur photographers she could not get our heads in focus. 'Never mind, that way Manuel can't recognize you,' she said to laugh away her fear. Both women were terrified that Manuel might appear on their doorstep. A few months before he had smashed up the shop of the man who had rescued Marcia.

Manuel had a reputation for extreme violence. Marcia told me, 'He had married an Argentinian woman in Germany. We heard he had maltreated her and had set her house on fire. She went missing, but to ward off suspicion he kept on sending money to her family. Rumour has it that he killed her.' The body of a dark woman was found around that time in Germany, but she was so badly burned that she could not be identified. Marcia and Ana have always been convinced the dead woman was Manuel's Argentinian first wife.

Ana had met Manuel in much the same way as Marcia. She remembered vividly her first meeting with him. 'He came to a rendezvous house for women who were looking for a husband. I was divorced and wanted to start a new life. I fell for him instantly. He even introduced himself to my parents as their future son-in-law. Later on I realized that he only did this to find out my parents' address so he could threaten them.' The marriage between Ana and Manuel was supposed to take place in Europe, but never happened because shortly after they arrived Ana discovered he was already married. This was a big shock to her because she really was in love with him. Much to her distress, her beloved threatened to kill her if she did not start working as a prostitute straight away. The couple went to Italy, where Ana had a bad time living in brothels. Next Manuel and she went to Spain, where she made a fruitless attempt to escape with a client. An associate of Manuel's, Julio, tracked down the customer and intimidated him. Ana was returned to Manuel, who gave Julio the task of guarding her.

Julio, Manuel and Ana went to the Netherlands, where she soon discovered that Manuel had several former fiancées working for him. She also found out that Manuel had a number of associates. Julio, whom she knew already, had to guard the women. He was helped by a bankrobber, who was ordered to marry one of the victims to keep her in the Netherlands. This man was considered very dangerous. There was also a madam in Utrecht, who employed the women and married off her own son to a victim in a bogus marriage. One of the gang members posed as a lawyer and collected the money from the women. He was at home in Colombian criminal circles and advised other traffickers. In the Italian mafia he would have been called a *consigliere*, an adviser. Ana said, 'All these scumbags knew each other. They said, even if you don't know us, we know everything about you. We keep an eye on you, even if you don't see us.'

Manuel had his own special ways of inspiring fear. One of Ana and Marcia's fellow victims had reported him to the police, but unfortunately one statement was insufficient to keep him in jail. He took this particular woman to a solicitor to make her retract her statement, but the solicitor refused to have anything to do with it. Manuel was furious. He took it out on the woman by putting her in the charge of a female Colombian killer, who sat by her all day, knife in hand.

For the women every escape route was blocked. Ana especially was threatened. Manuel put a flick knife to her throat several times and on one occasion killed her pet.

One day Marcia escaped with a client. She phoned Ana at work: 'Surprise, surprise, I escaped. Are you coming to congratulate me?' Ana didn't dare because Manuel would kill not only her but her family as well if she tried to run away. She didn't even dare to telephone for help. When Manuel heard Marcia had got away, he was so angry that he beat Ana up even more frequently than before. He also threatened to hurt her children. After a few months she could take no more. One day when he was out at the doctor's she called a taxi and went to Marcia, who put her up for a while.

Beyond the reach of the law

Though Manuel was originally from Colombia, he also had Spanish and German nationality. He had girls working for him in Germany and spoke German fluently. He owned a Porsche and had a Swiss bank account in which he deposited his takings. His group operated in a number of countries: Colombia, Germany, Argentina, the Dominican Republic and Italy.

It was a long time before Marcia and Ana dared to go to the police. They were deterred by the flood of threats coming from Manuel and his gang. When Marcia first talked to the police, Manuel was not under arrest and escaped to Colombia. He called Marcia from her parents' home to make it clear that he was quite prepared to carry out his threats. Marcia's mother came to the phone too, but Marcia didn't dare to warn her. When the women finally talked to the police they didn't have the courage to name all the group members involved. It was another few months before they were ready to bring everything into the open but the court decided there was a lack of evidence to have the case reopened.

Manuel is still globe-trotting. When Ana saw the documentary about Lisa's case, she wanted to organize a televised search for Manuel. This never came to anything because she had success-fully started a new life. She now has a good job and is happily married. Marcia does social work as a volunteer. The other girls who were involved were less fortunate. One of them underwent years of psychotherapy to help her recover.

Maria, Marcia and Ana were following in the footsteps of other Dominican and Colombian women, who had left their home countries in the 1970s and 1980s to seek their fortunes in the near-by wealthier Antilles. One of the Antillese islands had a reservation for prostitutes, Campo Alegre, where at first Colombian and Dominican women worked. After an influx of foreign prosti-tutes, Campo Alegre became too small. Those who wanted more space took to the streets or went abroad. Many of the women found Antillese men who had Dutch passports and were prepared to go through a marriage ceremony with them for payment. By this means the women became entitled to Dutch passports.[2] At the time such marriages were big business on the Caribbean island of Curaçao, a former Dutch colony, where their price was 15,000 guilders.[3] One Dutchman became rich by arranging 500 marriages.[4] After the wedding ceremony the women travelled to Europe, often accompanied by their husbands. The Colombian ex-prostitute Josephina, who came to Europe in the 1980s, said, 'When I arrived in the Netherlands, some ten years ago, there were already many Colombian women in Holland. Quite a few men forced their wives into prostitution and pocketed the proceeds.' Some women with Dutch passports also moved on to Germany or other European countries.

After 1985 the law on Dutch nationality was changed to prevent foreign women who married Antillese men from obtaining Dutch nationality. It then became cheaper for brothel-owners and potential traffickers to import Latin American women directly from the Dominican Republic and Colombia.

Dominican women are also trafficked to Panama, Venezuela and other Latin American countries. In the early 1980s many people were illegally transported from St Maarten to Puerto Rico and the United States. This ended tragically in 1985 when a number of women hidden in containers were found dead from asphyxiation.[5]

Cocaine

Whenever traffic in women by criminals from Colombia is discussed, the question of its relation to the drugs trade also comes up. One of the first cases of trafficking in Colombian women to the Netherlands, which occurred in 1984, involved cocaine. The main suspect was a transsexual who combined trafficking with trading in coke. He had promised some Colombian women jobs in a biscuit factory. According to his lawyer the transsexual trafficked in women and drugs to prove himself in the male-dominated drug scene. Women are sometimes trafficked by gangs who are also active drug dealers and occasionally Colombian prostitutes are forced to take part in the drugs trade. A former social worker, Ester Rios, said, 'I know a Latin American prostitute who met a gorgeous Argentinian at a dinner party. She liked him and was pleased when he invited her to visit his apartment in Spain. She went but he never turned up. Instead the police raided the place and found large quantities of cocaine. She was busted, not the Argentinian.' Three Colombian clients of STV who refused to co-operate in drug dealing were threatened. Prostitutes are often offered drugs to keep them going, but of STV's 500 clients over the last five years only two became addicts during their time as prostitutes. Finally, there are the women who are already addicts in their homeland who can easily become the victims of traffickers.

Manuel also made money from drug trafficking, but was never convicted of it. Marcia did not dare to bring this sideline of his to the police's attention. 'When Colombians talk too much their tongues are cut out. One telephone call to Colombia will do. What was I to say to the police? In Colombia there are gangs who traffic in both women and drugs. I know because my ex-husband in Colombia was involved in a gang. I could not talk about it there or here. My ex-husband's friends were mafiosi who were even worse than Manuel.'

Prostitution-related drug trafficking does not occur only in Colombia. Drugs, especially cocaine, are often part of sex clubs' trade. In some places doormen traffic drugs. If business is slack, some club managers make the women run drugs. Nowadays window brothels are centres for both the arms and drug trades.[6] Potential buyers pretend to be clients. The police are powerless because they are meant to respect the privacy of prostitutes and their clients.

At first the Dutch community was startled by the frequent occurrence of violence in Colombian circles, which is always the case when a new group appears on the scene. The Turkish gangs, which arrived next, were reputed to be extremely violent, but were soon surpassed by the sheer terror exercised by eastern European criminals.

7 Keeping it in the family[1]

One ingenious system used to traffic women from South America to Europe involved the creation of 'artificial families'. In the Netherlands, for example, a number of women had gained Dutch nationality by marrying Antillese men. Many of them were approached by traffickers to see if they would be willing to claim 'daughters' who had been given forged birth certificates and who would then qualify for Dutch nationality. A number of women agreed to take part in these 'artifical families', as they were called by the police. While some of the 'mothers' co-operated fully with the traffickers, others felt guilty and tried to help their 'daughters'.

Until 1987 children aged under 21 who had an Antillese parent with Dutch nationality could themselves opt for Dutch nationality. To obtain a Dutch passport they simply needed to produce their birth certificate. A Dominican gang exploited this law by providing women with false birth certificates and 'mothers', with the sole aim of taking the women to the Netherlands to force them into prostitution. The women's dates of birth were often falsified – in some cases the 'daughters' were actually the same age as their 'mothers'. By this method ten women could create 100 'daughters'. Their husbands, who had given them Dutch nationality, were not involved. The gang's operations worked so successfully that later on they also sent women to work in Germany.

Conchita's story

Conchita was one of the first women I met who had fallen into the hands of this gang. She told me about the scale of their fraud. She came from the Dominican Republic and became pregnant when she was 27. Neither she nor her family could take care of a baby. Her mother was in hospital and her deaf father already had to feed her ten brothers and sisters. She would have to give up her office job, so her problems were serious.

'One day I went to visit a friend who was going to a meeting to discuss job opportunities in Europe. I went with her and met a schoolteacher, who knew someone called Juan who could get me a job in the Netherlands. When I went to see him, his associates told me I would easily find employment in a beauty parlour. I asked whether my pregnancy posed a problem. "If you're having a baby you really should go, because in the Netherlands the queen and the government lay great value on the welfare of pregnant women," they told me. I thought Holland was a woman's paradise where no prostitution existed. Only later did I find out that most Dominican women in Europe were hookers.'

Juan recruited women in the Dominican Republic for the Belgian and Dutch prostitution markets, helped by his two sisters, who lived in the Netherlands. He was associated with a travel agency which lent tickets to women, which they used when applying for a visa at the Belgian embassy in Santo Domingo. He would also lend them showmoney. They went into the embassy on their own, but when they left he would immediately take the tickets and money back. For this he charged them £1,000. Juan was reputed to have excellent relations with the embassy: in 1994 the Belgian consul in the Dominican Republic was fired because he had contacts with a travel agency which helped women to go to Europe.

Conchita had to find her own showmoney and struggled to save the necessary amount. Next she was told she had to pay a large sum for the ticket, which her brother advanced to her on the assumption that she would come back a rich woman. 'I'll never dare to tell him why I can't pay the money back. Maybe he'll be discreet, but you never know. I don't want the rest of the family to know what happened to me.'

Finally Conchita set off for the feminist paradise on the North Sea. 'A woman whom I had seen at the meeting collected me from Brussels airport. I trusted her completely. After all, I thought she was the respectable owner of a beauty parlour. That's why I wasn't surprised when I had to pay £150 extra for the trip to the Netherlands.' This was far more than the normal price for a train ticket. However, Conchita could not use normal methods of transport because she was an illegal immigrant. She had to use the industry which has mushroomed to smuggle illegal immigrants over the so-called green borders, the unguarded crossings.

'With other people we went by car to the Netherlands. By then I had been travelling for days on end. I was exhausted. I told the others that because of my pregnancy the journey was very tiring. "What?" they cried. "Are you pregnant? If that's true, you are in for a whole lot of trouble." I told them that Juan had assured me my pregnancy wouldn't be a problem. But that was not the case. "When you have to go hospital, the doctors are bound to ask for your papers, which you don't have. They'll send you back home, pregnant or not." I was left feeling very disturbed.

'The evening I arrived in Amsterdam they showed me around the red light district. "This is the place where you'll have to work," they said. I began to cry, "My God, do I have to do this kind of work?" After that walk, at one o'clock at night, we went to the flat of the woman who had collected me from Brussels airport.

'I went straight to bed, but I couldn't sleep. When they thought I couldn't hear, they made jokes about my pregnancy. Even now they still hurt. I cried all night. The next day they said, "You'll have to make a decision. Either way you have to pay your debt, and you owe us money for your housing as well." I didn't know of any debt and I wanted to go home. I felt bad because it had cost me so much and I didn't even have a return ticket. If necessary, I thought I would pay my return fare myself. By then I knew I had paid them far too much for their so-called services.'

Fearing that she would run away, the women kept her under lock and key. 'In the Dominican Republic they never told me I could not go home. I felt cheated. I threatened to write a letter to the Dominican Republic to expose the fraud. They just laughed.

'I sat brooding for a couple of days. I thought, "I have been cheated, that is a fact, but what can I do? The Dominican women who live here won't report me to the police. I will endure it for a few months and then go home."

'It went against the grain, but after two days I went to the window they had arranged for me. The manager of the brothel, a Dominican woman, said, "Now that you are here, you have to sleep with the customers, otherwise you can't pay for the room." She looked after everything for the owner. She conned the proprietor of the windows because she only told him the earnings of three women, but she had eight girls working there. The proceeds of the other five went into her own pockets.

'I still remember my very first customer. Whatever he wanted, I refused. I cried my eyes out and told him I had never done that kind of work before. I also admitted to being pregnant. He left, but the next customers didn't buy this argument. I was scared to death, because another pregnant girl was beaten up by a client in the very same place.'

Conchita was not successful behind the windows but not knowing what else to do, she stayed on. Soon two other women came by and made her an offer she couldn't refuse. They sent her to another part of the country, where Conchita was told she would be working as a cleaner in a bar. 'When I arrived I started to clean the place. The manager said, "What do you think you are doing?" and made it clear that cleaning was not expected of me. I took to drinking that vinegar-like champagne.'

Conchita's new colleagues told her, 'You were a fool to leave the windows. Here you also have to work with men, but you make less money.' Conchita had hoped she would only have to drink with customers. Once again she didn't attract many customers and was fired.

She was now free but alone. She was pregnant, she had no money or return ticket and she knew nobody. She drifted until eventually she met a Latin American woman, who took her to a social worker who helped her. Her baby was born in a hospital after all. After a long time, she finally went to the police. No one was ever brought to trial.

Conchita found herself a husband and a nice flat. 'What more could I desire?' she said to me on one of the last times we met. She was to be denied her peace: one day in 1992 a Boeing crashed on the flat where she lived. She survived, but had to be rehoused. The crash was a major disaster and the queen came to inspect the damage. At last Conchita saw the queen, who was unaware of the abuse traffickers made of her reputation as the fairy queen of a feminist paradise.

Artificial families

The two women who took Conchita away from the windows to the club were friends of the manager. They collected Conchita's money and carried a knife, to make the situation quite clear. One of them was rumoured to have killed a man in the Dominican Republic. Conchita said, 'This woman had obtained Dutch nationality with a paper stating she was a daughter of Dominican and Antillese parents. That paper was a forgery.' Conchita was right. The woman had entered the Netherlands illegally through the system of 'artificial families'.

The gang which organized this scam was headed by two elderly Dominican sisters, helped by a son and daughter-in-law. So far they have trafficked over 100 women. One of the sisters, señoras as they were called by their victims, organized the forged papers in the Dominican Republic with the help of a corrupt civil servant. In the Dominican Republic the authorities don't keep exact records of birth certificates and it is relatively easy to obtain false documents. The señora who ran that end of the operation was so good at organizing the paperwork that she was nicknamed the consul. The other sister, who ran the business in the Netherlands, befriended Dominican women who had obtained Dutch nationality by marriage and were willing to pretend to be 'mothers' to the 'daughters'.

The elderly señoras managed to recruit a lot of women because they were able to convince them of their good intentions. They concentrated on women they already knew, indeed some of their victims had been acquainted with the señoras for years: they were only too ready to believe the elderly ladies when they said they could arrange jobs in a Dutch factory. One girl had been a domestic worker for the señora, who had kindly given her the job when she fled from her violent husband. Another woman was asked to join the señoras by an old schoolfriend. A few girls were promised other employment. Victoria, aged 27, was told she would qualify for a student grant in the Netherlands. 'The señora said she would see to it that I could finish my studies. I already knew the señora when I was a child. She lived with one of our acquaintances. Before taking me abroad, the señora had a long talk with my father. But she refused to say where I was going to live. That's why at first my father didn't want to let me go. But in the end she convinced him she had contacts in high places.' Victoria told me all this the first time I spoke to her at her hideout, which was a small room with only a bed.

Victoria saw no reason to mistrust the señora and so went to the Netherlands with her. 'When we arrived there she suddenly seemed a different person. I felt frightened, and with reason. I had to get a passport on which I was somebody else, with a new name and a different age. A few days later the señora told me I had to pay her £15,000, which was an enormous amount of money for me. She also said I could only earn that kind of money behind the windows. She said if I didn't comply I would be in big trouble and she pointed out that I didn't have papers showing my own age and name. She was right. I knew I was in the wrong and it had a bad psychological effect on me. I didn't know who I was any more. Would I have to live under another name for the rest of my life? I was afraid that I would never have my own passport again.' Victoria didn't think of going to the police, who would inevitably expose her fake identity. 'But I found it reassuring that there were other Dominican women living under a false name who were saddled with debts like mine.'

There seemed to be no way out and Victoria headed for the red light district. She had never been a prostitute, which was true of many other artificial daughters. Some of them were planted behind the windows on the day they arrived, but not Victoria. 'My first few days in the Netherlands I was ill with the flu. I had to start work a few weeks later. I only had Sundays off. The señora's niece taught me the tricks of the trade. It was the other girls who told me about AIDS. I didn't need AIDS on top of everything else, so I always made the clients use a condom. The work was difficult: even if you had a headache or felt out of sorts, you still had to be nice to the punters to get your daily ratio.

'There wasn't a telephone in the studio space, so I couldn't call anyone. I never went out on the streets because I was afraid someone would recognize me and report me as an illegal immigrant.'

Victoria only worked in one city. Other girls had to commute between several red light districts. Members of the gang accompanied them to the brothels or arranged for other people to take them. One woman only found out afterwards where she had worked. 'Have I been to Rotterdam?' she asked. She never knew for sure. According to Victoria the señoras had many helpers who prevented the women from running away or speaking to anyone. Members of the gang collected the women's earnings and checked up on them daily. The women had to pay for everything, including unpacking their own suitcases. The señora even charged them for the use of a bed in her home. Part of this money disappeared into an informal banking system called the *san*. *Sans* are quite common in the Dominican Republic and are a method of avoiding official banks. The funds of the *san* are controlled by rotating chairpersons: both legitimate and illegal money can be invested in them and relatively cheap loans are available. The señora used the *san* for loan-sharking. A minority of the women who didn't earn enough money were forced to borrow from the señora's *san*. The longer it took them to pay off their instalments, the higher the interest they owed. One girl even had to pay 50 per cent interest, while others were paying 10 per cent. For the gang this was just a little side earner; the big money came from prostitution. When everybody was 'working', the señoras were making at least £1,000 every two hours, a witness told me. The gang was making millions of pounds, but its members were not conspicuous consumers. They lived in a council house in the Netherlands and didn't even own a VCR. According to one of the girls, they took a suitcase crammed with bank notes to the Dominican Republic every week. The police have never been able to trace this money.

Victoria broke down after she had paid back £1,500. 'I told the señora that I was not going to pay £15,000 for a false name and a false passport. In her turn the señora threatened again to tell the police that I had stolen passports. But by then I had come to realize the señora wouldn't dare because her part in the affair would inevitably come to light.' Instead of reporting Victoria to the police, the señora sent her son to beat her up, which he was unable to do. 'I could avoid him, but the other girls were less fortunate.' Talking about the other Dominican women in her group, Victoria became indignant. 'When they failed to pay up, their clothes were taken away and they were turned out in the cold.' One girl was left naked in the bushes after a row with the son.

None of the girls was said to have been raped and one 'artificial mother' even prevented her 'daughter' from being sexually assaulted. However, another 'mother' forced her ready-made 'daughter' to have an abortion because she would not attract enough customers if she were pregnant. The girl didn't want to give up the baby; because of an illness she had had it was her last chance to become pregnant. But there was no one she could tell. The señora went with her to the abortion clinic, which was legal, to make sure she kept her mouth shut. The girl even had to pay the clinic's fees herself.

The women were threatened all the time. When one woman said that she wouldn't mind dying, a member of the gang told her, 'Then we'll kill your parents and your children in the Dominican Republic. We'll set their house alight. And don't think you will ever be safe when you go home.' That was sufficient to frighten the women. Because of these threats and because they had false papers, the women did not dare to go to the police. A few of them had already paid for the false papers in the Dominican Republic and they were afraid that they would be accused of being accomplices.

The investigation and trial

The gang had become too greedy. To make the enterprise more profitable, the señoras invented a number of pairs of twins. This overcame the problem that an 'artificial mother' could only claim to have had one daughter every nine months. The statistics showed that 40 per cent of the young people who had opted for Dutch nationality were twins – an unnaturally high percentage, which alerted the police. By then some 70 'artificial families' had been created in the Netherlands. As a sideline, the gang also produced some 'artificial sons', by taking money off young men who wanted Dutch nationality.

Victoria was persuaded to go to the police by an Antillese boy who sold illegal lottery tickets and she only dared to come out of hiding because he gave her a place to stay. He also bought food for her and never took advantage of her. He was a true friend. Still, it took Victoria a long time to take the final step. 'I was afraid I would endanger my colleagues who had children and who were in an even more difficult situation than me.'

'Just after my arrival I was on friendly terms with the other girls. But as soon as they realized I didn't intend to pay the rest of the £15,000, their attitude changed completely. At first we all had our meals together, but after my first contact with the police I had to avoid the others, who were too close to the señora. I had to eat all by myself.' Victoria didn't dare go out on the streets because the gang knew she had made a statement to the police. 'It was a nuisance, but as soon you poke your nose outside, they know where to find you. Except with my Antillese friend, I had no contacts with outsiders. After I had been heard by the examining magistrate, I only spoke to the officers at the police station, where I was put up for my own safety. I couldn't meet my former colleagues any more.'

During their investigations, the police did not act solely on the evidence of the large numbers of twin births, but worked from tip-offs as well. Previously in trafficking cases they had not listened to criminal informants, but had waited for women to come forward. Chief Inspector Van Loon and Detective Kroos, who at the time were in charge of the investigation, said, 'In the technicalities of policing, traffic in women comes between rape and drug trafficking. In cases of rape we only have the stories of victims who confide in the police. In drug cases, on the other hand, an addict never gives evidence against a dealer. In policing traffic in drugs we have to rely completely on signals coming out of the milieu. Unfortunately, this method of network investigation is very expensive. This case has cost more than half a million pounds.'

Victoria, together with nine other girls, gave the police more than enough evidence to bring a case. The outcome was that one middle-aged lady and some gang members were brought to trial in 1989. They were sentenced to two to three years in jail. The other señora, the sister who took care of the business in the Dominican Republic, could not be extradited to the Netherlands. The court case took place with many of the trafficked women muttering angrily in the public gallery. They took turns to take care of their children, who were playing on the court house stairs. Because he knew the victims were present, the son of one of the señoras played to the gallery. He kept turning round to eye the women from the dock, while flaunting his indifference to the judge. When the judge asked him what he did for a living, he answered, 'I was remanded in custody, so the state provided for me. I was also paid to help move the girls from one place to another. I hustled on the side and I was on the dole.'

Judge: 'You also travelled to the Dominican Republic and our rogatory commission by now knows how expensive these trips are.'

Son: 'I paid with the money the girls had given me to keep in a safe place.'

Judge: 'You mean prostitution money?'

Son: 'I have so much esteem for you and the respectable married women present in the court room that I dare not answer this question in public.'

This remark provoked much laughter in the public gallery.

Judge: 'Let me ask you again whether you lived on prostitution money.'

Son: 'You might logically conclude that.'

Judge: 'Did you tell the women they could only work in the sex industry?'

Son: 'I just told them that all women work in prostitution.'

The judge then asked what had happened to the woman who was left stark naked in the bushes.

Son: 'You shouldn't overdo it. It wasn't a fully fledged wood, just a small shrubbery.'

His mother, the señora, defended herself. 'My sister in the Dominican Republic advances the money for the tickets. She is a smart woman. I am falsely accused by these girls. One of them was a qualified seamstress and could have worked as such. They are just jealous because I live quietly on my own money.'

The judge said, 'You have real estate in the Dominican Republic.' The women in the public gallery hissed, 'Bought with our money.' The señora refused to admit that she had taken the money from the women and denied threatening them. As a woman and mother herself, she would never do that, she claimed. The group were also charged with being members of a criminal organization. This charge failed because the judge would not equate family relationships with organized crime.

After the trial

As soon as the gang leaders had been sent to prison, some of the women went back to work as prostitutes. They didn't dare to go home penniless. After all, they had come to Europe to support their families and prostitution was the only profession open to them. They worked 'illegally' because their temporary permits didn't entitle them to have a normal job. As Conchita had found, some of the women became traffickers themselves.

Victoria eventually overcame her fear of going out in the street alone, but she never returned to prostitution. She found herself a regular job because she had a permanent residence permit. Soon after the trial she married. Unfortunately her husband abused her and spent the money she had to work for so hard. She divorced him and he was deported to the Dominican Republic soon afterwards, where he was killed in a quarrel between criminals.

Victoria's new life didn't last long. In 1994 I received the sad news that she had died in a traffic accident. Her death was investigated thoroughly and the police concluded that she had not been murdered. Nevertheless, her misfortune fed rumours that she had been killed. Word travels fast in Dominican circles.

While he was in prison the son managed to write a threatening letter to one of the women who had pressed charges against him. For this he was refused parole. For all the gang members their prison sentences were only an interruption to their criminal activities. The señora's son is reputed to be continuing his business in Germany with a Spanish partner, an outsider to the family.

After the señora was released it was rumoured that she specialized in the marriage racket. 'She is recruiting women in the Antilles. In the meantime she still draws social security as in the old days,' Josephina, the independent prostitute from Colombia, told me. Some gang members are trying to set up in business in the United States, which they enter by way of Mexico to avoid the obligatory visa. Some women in the Netherlands are being forced to pay for the lawyers the gang have hired to legalize their stay in the United States.

Most of the 'artificial mothers' were let off and some started a business on their own. One woman recruited a girl who had to use her false passport to become her 'daughter-in-law'. One 'artificial daughter' was made to use her illegally obtained passport to marry a relative of the señoras, so he would obtain a residence permit. One 'artificial mother' forced her real goddaughter to get a false birth certificate which showed her as the 'mother'. The girl didn't dare to oppose her own godmother, who was middle-aged and paid a lawyer in the Dominican Republic to arrange everything. When her 'artificial daughter' went to the police some time later, no case could be brought because too much time had elapsed. This also happened to other women and the police expelled most of those who had false papers.

Former 'artificial daughters' kept surfacing until 1994. They had to. They had been on the dole for years and had used their false passports to apply for social security. They were uncovered by detectives investigating fraud. In most cases the social security money went straight into the pockets of the gang members and their associates. Now many of the women are sorry they didn't come forward earlier. Others have disappeared, like Clarita, who had to hand her social security money over to her 'artificial mother'. Moreover, Clarita had to pay off the loans her 'mother' had taken out in her name. She was terrified of this woman, who had reputedly killed two men in the Dominican Republic, and didn't dare to give evidence. Clarita had also heard that women who had pressed charges had found themselves in a lot of trouble. She preferred to go back to the Dominican Republic.

The loophole in Dutch law by which artificial families were created has now been closed, but these families are not exclusively a Dutch problem. According to the London lawyer Jean Gould, there are Latin American groups in the United Kingdom who pull the same trick. It is unclear whether or not their 'artificial kin' are exploited in prostitution.

Other artificial families

Fraud in family relations is not new. In 1987 two men from Rotterdam were arrested because they adopted foreign people. They 'helped out' illegal aliens without passports with hand-typed false adoption papers, drafted by non-existent solicitors. They arranged for paid adoptive parents. They conducted their business in pubs, but it was never established that this was done for the purposes of prostitution.[2]

Leslie Roberts of the London branch of the International Anti-Slavery Society said, 'In Britain there is the odd example of false adoption. Local authorities don't have the services to vet the adopted children. I am sure people come in on false invitations, but we don't know whether that is a ploy to manipulate women into prostitution.'

It is still theoretically possible to set up fraudulent families by falsely claiming children. A European tourist can easily go to the Dominican Republic and claim to have fathered a girl many years before on holiday, in order to bring her back to Europe and turn her out on the streets.

Leen Pieterse of the Criminal Intelligence Unit said, 'In those cases an alleged father has to go to great lengths to prove himself. We know of these methods, but we haven't heard of any cases. I would have known if it occurred frequently, and by frequently I mean four or five times a year. The embassy personnel are alerted. Besides, it would attract the attention of other authorities.'

8 The Greek connection

Greece has a tradition of trafficking in women. In the 1960s men were leaving the countryside for the cities to find employment. To meet an increasing demand for prostitutes, girls were recruited in rural areas, often with false job promises, and forced onto the game. The number of girls arriving in urban centres was matched by the increase in the number of pimps. Unemployment in Greece then forced many men to look for work in western and northern Europe. A minority of them were criminals.[1] Among other things, they became involved in trafficking women from South America and eastern Europe.

In the Netherlands Greek traffickers were helped by the ease with which an entertainer's visa could be obtained. The Dutch authorities handed out these visas liberally to anyone who wanted to hire artistic performers. For years Greece had been an important distribution centre for go-go dancers, and in the 1980s both Greece and Cyprus played major roles in the international trade in such dancers, who had entertainers' visas. Before 1987 abuse of this system was unknown, but by 1992 the Dutch police were saying, 'We don't know if they are being used for trafficking in women, but there is certainly a massive transfer of prostitutes.' The authorities have become more careful about who they issue the visas to since this method of recruitment received bad publicity.

Ester Rios, a social worker in the Netherlands who helped trafficked as well as non-trafficked South American prostitutes, said in 1991 that among the 150 regular visitors to her centre there were at least ten dancers who had been exploited by traffickers and pimps in Greece. Three of them, Celestina, Hermana and Viola, describe their odyssey through the Greek underworld later in this chapter.[2] Among the first women to come to the authorities' notice as being trafficked by Greeks were Tonia and Natalie.

In 1992 two Greek brothers reported to the Dutch police the theft of two Bulgarian girls by a Dutchman. This strange complaint was investigated and eventually officers found the women, who were overjoyed. The 'thief' turned out to be a punter who had rescued Tonia and Natalie from window prostitution. The brothers were brought to trial and the women were called as witnesses. They said it had all started when they had gone from Bulgaria to Hungary on holiday. In a Budapest café they met the brothers, who invited them on a short trip to Germany. When they arrived in Düsseldorf, instead of enjoying a holiday, they were kept prisoner in a two-room apartment. The brothers made Tonia sleep with their friends, who then paid the brothers. These friends were a taxi driver, a restaurant owner and a waiter in the restaurant. Natalie was better off: 'One of the brothers was in love with me and reserved me for himself. I was taken out once in a while. I noticed they did something to my friend Tonia. At the time I didn't realize what was happening, but I heard her screaming and crying. She was kept in a separate room. We were not allowed to speak to each other.' Next the two women were taken to the red light district in Amsterdam. They were both afraid because the brothers were well armed.

At the trial the Greeks' friends were called as witnesses for the defence and they all testified that the women were professional prostitutes who had obviously enjoyed sexual relations with several men. The taxi driver said he had met the girls by chance while his car was being repaired at a garage. The restaurant owner bragged that the women had taken him and the waiter to the cellar to have sex with them after dinner. Most of their evidence contained blatant contradictions. 'All these Greeks in Düsseldorf know each other,' the two women commented indignantly. They were right. The stories were obviously inventions and the witnesses were charged with perjury and locked away.

However, the trial then took a strange turn. Tonia, who had said she was kept prisoner in Düsseldorf, was also accused of perjury. In Germany a neighbour of the brothers, who had no relationship with them, was positive she had seen Tonia outside. An independent kiosk owner said the same thing. A year after the event these two witnesses had managed to recognize her from a small passport photo. Since it was impossible to prove that the two were not impartial witnesses, Tonia and Natalie were also convicted of perjury. The Greek brothers and their friends were released from jail and even sued the Department of Justice successfully for damages. Tonia and Natalie have appealed against this conviction but the appeal has not yet come to court.

The traffic in entertainers

A slender girl dances onstage. Slowly she undresses to the sound of reggae music. A busload of tourists wait for her next act: writing 'Greetings from Amsterdam' with her lower body. Nowadays every sex club worthy of the name features a dance act like this. They became popular when old-fashioned night clubs with variety acts became unfashionable and audiences began to demand live sex and not just striptease. Finding able dancers is difficult, so managers of sex clubs make do with their own employees, who are reluctant to comply because they are seldom paid any extra.

Entertainment agencies (and there are several which supply dancers with skills like writing with their private parts) try to fill the gap with cheap, untrained, migrant performers. The dancer who performed the 'Greetings from Amsterdam' act is from former Yugoslavia, according to the doorman at the theatre, which features live sex as well. 'We also employ a Colombian dancer,' he said.

The dancers at this particular theatre are probably working on entertainers' visas. The contracts offered to them by the impresarios are 'informal', so abuse for prostitution is easy. A few 'imported cultural dancers' think they have been hired to perform traditional dances. Instead they have to undress and, once trapped, more often than not are also forced to have sexual intercourse with clients.

Several hundred go-go dancers were recruited in Greece. Josephina, the Colombian hooker who knows a great deal about 'foreigners' prostitution circles, said, 'Since I arrived in Holland some ten years ago, I have heard stories about Greece. At the time, Dutch sex-club owners paid commission to impresarios based in Greece, who sent girls to Holland.' For instance, Maria, a pregnant woman who was raped by her trafficker, was ordered by post for the Netherlands via Greece. Many migrant girls from eastern Europe are prostituting themselves in Greece. According to an Interpol report in 1988, 1,200 Ethiopian girls were working in Greek brothels. Brazilians are also thought to be trafficked by a Greek network.[3]

'I wanted to get more out of life'

Celestina, Hermana and her sister Amada came from the Dominican Republic and were all, at different times, victims of a gang run by Papa C. Celestina, who is 22, described herself as *pequeña*, small, but not too small. For safety reasons she didn't consort with Dominican women who knew many other Dominicans. She was afraid her whereabouts would become known in the tight-knit Dominican community in the Netherlands.

Hermana, on the contrary, was a big muscular woman who didn't care about her safety. She was too angry. 'I'll tell it all because I want something to be done about Papa C.' She spoke for her sister Amada as well, who had gone through similar experiences. 'Papa C. took the money my family needed so badly. And he has never stopped cheating Dominican women.' Taking into consideration the time that elapsed between Celestina and Hermana's experiences (Celestina's in the late 1980s and Hermana and Amada's in 1993), Papa C. must have been trafficking for at least five years. He was one of many agents operating in Greece.

All three women, Celestina, Hermana and Amada, had been job hunting in the Dominican Republic. Hermana had to earn her living because her husband was working in Portugal and didn't send enough money home. She and Amada were contacted by an intermediary, whom they met only once and who promised them jobs in Greece. Celestina was more definite about her agents: 'I told a friend that I wanted to get more out of life. He introduced me to two Dominican men who said they could help me out. I thought they were normal business executives.' The women were given the choice between working as dancers, waitressing in a Greek restaurant or being a receptionist. 'Now I realize that this intermediary knew the intentions of these two men. I never want to see him again,' Celestina said to me. At the time she chose to be a waitress. When Hermana applied it was for a job as a receptionist in a tourist office.

The women were given six-month contracts which promised them enormous salaries by Dominican standards. The sum they had to pay the agency was also huge in their eyes: 3,000 pesos. Celestina boarded the plane for Athens with twelve other girls. 'Three men were waiting for us at Athens airport. They said, "Oh, you are here for Papa C., please give us your passports." The other girls and I were frightened out of our wits when we got them back – with different names and ages. Only the photographs were genuine. They kept our genuine passports.' The men at the airport played the same trick on Hermana and her 20 travel companions.

After they reached Athens, Hermana and the others with her travelled to a seaside resort to the so-called tourist office. 'We had to start that very same day at eight o'clock in the evening. We thought it was strange. What tourist office opens up at that hour?' The moment the women entered the night club they realized their position. There was no escape. Hermana said, 'That first night I was like a piece of furniture. Punters could only look at me, not touch me. I didn't want to do that kind of work. Why would I do my best to attract customers? Surely not to line the pockets of the bosses. Later on I only had intercourse with men if I couldn't avoid it. And those customers smelled. I continually argued about money with this self-styled impresario, the proprietor of the club. Since I couldn't refuse customers, I wanted to be paid for entertaining them.'

After three months Hermana and her sister went to the Greek police. 'We didn't tell them everything because we were afraid for the girls we had left behind. We hoped the police would send us back to the Dominican Republic, but they couldn't do anything without our documents. So we went back to the agent. We threatened to call the police if he didn't give us our passports back within three weeks. Instead of returning them, he said, "Relax, everything will be OK." But he wanted to get rid of us and shoved us off to Papa C., who had apparently already paid commission for us. The recruiter in the Dominican Republic also worked for him and had arranged with our first boss to sell us on to Papa C. That first boss, the night-club owner, was a bastard, but Papa C. was worse.'

Papa C.

When she arrived in Greece Celestina was sent straight to Papa C., whom she described as 'an unpleasant and very bossy man'. She and her colleagues were put up in a hotel, which they could only leave if they asked the porter to accompany them. 'For the first few months we were not allowed out by ourselves. I never dared to complain to the punters, because it meant trouble if Papa C. heard of it. Besides, you didn't know if the customer was one of his spies.

'In the daytime we received thorough dance training. At night we had to perform in a night club. No matter how often we asked, we were never given our salary. Papa C. took everything from us, really everything. He lived in an enormous house, and one room was packed with luggage he had confiscated from the girls.'

Neither Celestina nor Hermana were beaten up by Papa C., but Hermana said, 'Other girls were. He had relationships with some of the women. When his wife found out, she treated the girls badly, although she knew perfectly well she couldn't stop his womanizing. She was scared to death of him. The others told me that she used to work for him too. She was Greek. We had to call her Mama Maria.' Celestina knew her too. 'I never called her Mama Maria. Others implored her, "Mama or Papa, please help me so and so." Not me. I was too proud for that.'

After a couple of months the regime became less strict because by then the women knew there was nowhere they could go. If they made problems, Papa C. simply moved them to another club. They couldn't leave because their visas had expired. 'I don't know if he had struck a deal with the local police,' Celestina said.

Many women stayed with Papa C. or committed suicide. One girl was said to have thrown herself off the balcony of Papa C.'s hotel, but some said they saw him push her. Papa C. told the police that she had jumped, and they believed him. This particular story was still being told when Hermana and her sister worked for Papa C. He obviously fostered its telling to discourage resistance from the women. However, the story had the opposite effect on Hermana and Amada. 'When we heard that, we thought we had to get away immediately.' Another woman in Hermana's group disappeared in the mountains and was never seen again. At that time they were marooned at Papa C.'s, who didn't bother to lock them up any more. He had learned over the years that fear alone was a cheap and efficient weapon which kept dancers from running away.

Hermana and her sister went to the Greek police for a second time. At the very least they hoped the police would help them to get their luggage back. 'The local police gave us a letter to Papa C. urging him to return our belongings. Of course we never dared to give it to him. We thought it better not to go back to Papa C.'s at all. Afterwards we sat on the stairs of the police station for hours. We met an Argentinian woman there who was in the last days of her pregnancy. She had a large belly and a very big heart. She gave us the money for our train fares to Athens. It was a long journey; on the way we almost starved to death.

'In Athens we went to the police again. We had heard that Athens had the greatest police force in the world.' Hermana expected too much of them. 'The policemen there asked if we had a job. "Yes," we said, and that was the end of the matter. They could not deport us because we were tied down by an employment contract. In Greece illegal immigrants have to pay for their return tickets. If they don't have the money, they have to pay for it working in jail.

'We were desperate. Eventually we phoned the Argentinian woman we had met. She sent a friend of hers, a Chilean, who arranged for us to get customers. We did not really want that, but we didn't know how to survive otherwise. We wanted to leave Greece immediately, to get away from Papa C. This Chilean gave us some clothes and let us live in his apartment. He also introduced us to someone who supplied us with false identity papers.'

The streetwise Chilean became their tour operator. He first sent Hermana and her sister to Italy, where a friend of his took care of them. This man sent the two women to another business associate, who in turn introduced them to Italian street life. In Italy nobody forced them to prostitute themselves and the women found their own housing. They managed to save enough money to buy a ticket to the Netherlands, where another 'friend' fed them and gave them the money to pay for a room in a Dutch hotel for a couple of days. This friend turned out to be a pimp who put the sisters back on the game.

Celestina runs away

Celestina did not go to the Greek police. She arrived in the Netherlands by a different route. After a few months Papa C. packed her off to one of his partners in crime, Dimitri, who was also an 'artists' agent'. She said 'The journey was terrible. I had to make a bus journey which lasted for several hours. I only saw mountains. When I finally arrived it turned out that Papa C. had given me the wrong address. After a lot of telephone calls and even more bus rides I finally arrived at Dimitri's.'

Celestina never had a sexual relationship with Papa C., but she did have an affair with Dimitri. 'He fell in love with me. He was a bit of a softie, but at least he had a heart. As I was involved with Dimitri, Papa C. didn't dare to thwart me any more. Dimitri was married to Carmen, a Dominican woman, who was also a prostitute. By the way, he also trafficked women himself. He recruited girls from the Dominican Republic and Chile for his own sex clubs in Greece. My intimacy with Dimitri gave me enough courage to quarrel with him. I demanded that we, the girls, should get the money, not Papa C. So he gave it to me and I shared it with the girls. They thought me very brave.'

Because of her behaviour, Celestina was no longer seen as a model of obedience. She had to go. Against his better judgment, Dimitri sent her to Athens, where she was supposed to contact a Rotterdam agent. 'Dimitri advanced me the train fare. I had to report to a hotel of Papa C.'s in Athens. I never went. Instead of following their timetable, I spent the rest of the money on a taxi to the nearest railway station.

'I ended up in Germany. I didn't know where to go and so I called a friend of Dimitri's in Holland. He sent a taxi to collect me. It wasn't very far because I was near to the Dutch border. Dimitri had told me that his friend was an ordinary family man who owned a restaurant, but I soon found out that he expected me to work in his escort service which he operated on the side. I escaped with a so-called client, who got me a job in an Amsterdam striptease joint. Stripping wasn't so hard to do. Nobody bothered me and the managers paid me what they owed me. I shut my eyes to their criminal activities. They were involved in the kidnapping of Heineken, the beer magnate, you know.' Soon Celestina became pregnant. Later she gave up her job to care for her daughter full-time.

'Do you believe my story?' she asked me at the end of our first meeting. She was very surprised when I told her that she was not the only victim of Papa C. to find herself stranded in the Netherlands.

Cyprus

Papa C. sent some of his women to Cyprus, which had been a transit post for prostitutes for a long time.[4] However, until a few years ago, nobody had examined the role of Cypriot agents in the international trade in women. The connections were played down as coincidental.

In the 1950s and 1960s Cyprus was an important distribution centre for white girls being sent to the Middle East. In the early 1960s the English journalist Sean O'Callaghan met a girl in one of Tripoli's night clubs.[5] She told him the following story. 'A few years ago I left England to go to Cyprus with some other dancers.

As we were quite successful as dancers we wanted to move on to Athens. So we went, but our manager left us in the lurch. Without his help we couldn't find a suitable place to work. I flew back to Cyprus with two other girls, but the situation had changed overnight in the old club. We were told we would be sacked if we refused to sleep with the clients. We met a man there who invited us to go and work in Beirut. We accepted, but that was even worse. It was a private night club where they beat us up and made us go without food.' She could not escape. Instead she had to help a Frenchman to recruit other girls in various European cities. He told the girls that they were wasting their talents and that he could offer them better opportunities.

The English girl, in the meantime, had found out she had become part of a notorious 'syndicate', which had at least 19 members and worked with procurers in European and Arab countries, recruiting through artists' agencies. The head of the syndicate, who was brought to trial in the Lebanon in 1964, was one Hassan Ali Karim. O'Callaghan checked out the English girl's story by posing as an undercover trafficker. He heard reports of women who had been drugged and detained in luxurious harems. Other girls, who had started off in dance groups, ended up in night clubs and brothels. John Keet, the manager of an agency, described his methods to O'Callaghan: 'A girl is hired as a dancer for a realistic fee, and is reported missing afterwards.'

English ballet dancers were supposed to be in particular danger because they were favourites with men in northern Africa and the Middle East. English girls could be found working in most of Beirut's 500 night clubs. A classic example of trafficking at that time was the Champagne Ballet in Cyprus, which was run by an English woman who recruited schoolgirls through an agency in Sheffield. The girls were offered a contract with a no-play no-pay stipulation. At first they were employed in the wardrobe department, where they invariably became extremely bored. By this time, they were ready to drink with the customers. The next step was for the night-club manager to promise them a better job in the Middle East.

Modern agents adapted this existing infrastructure for trafficking women, but the women weren't being sent east any more but to western Europe instead. They also catered for the local market, for the many soldiers who were based in Cyprus.[6]

A notorious Cypriot called Ernesto B. operated in the late 1980s. A Frenchman called Vladimir A. had supplied the clubs in

Rotterdam with Thai girls trained in Cyprus.[7] Vladimir had started this trade in Cyprus. Later he supplied the Belgians, who were known as the Billionaire gang, with so-called dancers. Ernesto B., himself of Lebanese origin, was well connected in the Lebanon. One of the women who was sold by Ernesto to the Billionaire gang was sent to the Lebanon, an old Middle East destination for trafficked women.

Unhampered by the civil war, traffic to the Lebanon continued during the 1980s. Despite the presence of the so-called Terry Waite watchers, who were monitoring the captivity of the archbishop of Canterbury's envoy, many agents brought Filipinas into the Lebanon with the help of corrupt immigration officers.

Flora from the Philippines, the domestic helper whose story is told in chapter 13, was employed in the Lebanon at the time. 'I would never work as a stripper, but I befriended a dancer who had run away from her employer. That's why I offered her a place to sleep in my house. The bosses of the dancers came after her. They formed a mafia-like organization which also traded drugs.' According to Flora, Philippine President Aquino repatriated many dancers when the bombing intensified. They were given priority over domestic helpers, who were housed with their employers. Three hundred domestic workers were abandoned and had to become prostitutes in order to survive.[8] Other 'entertainers' were sent back to the Philippines via Syria. Flora learned that many of them were exported to work in Belgium and Luxemburg. Domestic workers who successfully fled from the Lebanon were offered jobs by middlemen as 'cultural dancers' in Cyprus.

Viola, aged 26, from Colombia, was sent to Cyprus by Ernesto B.'s organization. She told her story reluctantly. 'Cyprus was teeming with agencies. Impresarios worked with cabaret proprietors. We never found out exactly who was involved. Personally I didn't have much to do with Ernesto, I only saw him once or twice. The bosses distanced themselves from the cabaret girls. I only knew that Ernesto was married to a Spanish woman and consequently spoke Spanish perfectly. Our agency alone had some 20 staff members.' During our conversation she referred to the agency staff vaguely as 'them'. 'My dancing group consisted of twelve girls.' The dancing groups were organized by nationality. Viola said, 'There were ballets from Argentina, Colombia and Thailand. I also met girls from El Salvador.'

Viola was recruited by the Colombian branch of Ernesto B.'s organization. 'In Colombia a friend took me to a hotel, where a Spanish businessman and his associates were holding a reception. They were ordinary men – actually they were quite nice. The Spanish man said he was looking for a professional dancer, which I wasn't, but he offered to get me training and promised me an artistic career. I even had to pass an audition of sorts.

'I found out later they needed no fewer than ten girls. The impresario employed everyone. I thought to myself, "Something is wrong. Don't do it," so I told him I had only contacted him out of curiosity and I had decided not to take up his offer. He went to a lot of trouble to persuade me. "We operate on a completely legal basis and we will give you a contract." I was promised £350 a month, money I could really do with. That sounded better, so I decided to give it a go after all.'

Viola flew to Athens with eight other girls. 'A man was waiting for us at the airport and he asked us if we were the Colombians he was expecting. When we said yes, he immediately confiscated our papers and passports. Then he took us to a hotel. We were supposed to start dancing the very next evening. "Regular dancing", they had told us,' Viola added ironically, 'but with an unusual type of costume.'

Viola's first stop was in Piraeus, the port of Athens. There she stripped in clubs called the Crazy Horse and the Copacabana. 'We were never trained as dancers, we only had to learn to move sexily. I also had to wear make-up, which I hated. You know me, have you ever seen me wearing make-up? We were also told that as "artists" we had to entertain the customers. "Why?" we asked. "That's not why we came here." But they claimed we each had to earn £1,500 to pay back what we owed them.

'The first weeks we received no salary at all, just some food. We cooked our own meals, but they did the shopping, so we could dance full time. In between, when we were hungry and cold, we didn't get anything at all. We were often shivering because we were not allowed to wear trousers. We never had any time off, not even on official holidays. We couldn't talk among ourselves because the *chef de ballet* was always around. If we tried to he would separate us at once. We were all in the same situation and none of us spoke Greek. By the way, the *chef de ballet* was gay and didn't harass us. He took us to work and picked us up afterwards.

'After a month they gave us a few dollars to buy our own food. We spent it on the lottery in a desperate attempt to make some money. One of us had become involved with a Greek guy and wanted to leave. She asked for her passport but they wouldn't give it to her. We realized then that none of us would ever get our papers back. Another girl became so angry that she punched the *chef de ballet*. "You've deceived us," she said.

'Our bosses sent us to Cyprus next with the *chef de ballet*. We lived in a filthy old house owned by the organization, which we had to clean ourselves. There was only one bath for all those girls. Again they locked us up in our rooms. Since we had to repay the fare for our boat trip, we weren't paid a penny for months. In Cyprus we were forced to sleep with clients. We could not refuse a customer who wanted us for the whole night. Officially we could say no, but then we would never get any money.

'The bosses didn't give us condoms and we had no idea where or how to get them ourselves. No matter how much we were crying, the customers made us sit with them. I couldn't speak to them because they were mostly Greeks and Arabs. We had to drink with them before we slept with them. It wasn't long before we started to ask for alcohol ourselves. Soon I became an alcoholic. Once a drunken girl hit a customer. He hit her back so hard that she was badly hurt and I pleaded with the boss to let her go to the hospital. He refused and beat me up instead.'

Viola spent 18 months in Cyprus. 'One day we heard that a new group of Filipinas had arrived. They were young and beautiful, and some were still virgins. They didn't need us any more. The manager returned our passports and said, "Get out." At last we got some money. In all those months we had only earned £1,000.' Viola burst out crying and we had to stop our conversation for a while.

Though Viola was free, her misery wasn't over. 'Just before I heard I could go, Maria, a former girlfriend of Ernesto's, talked to me. I told her about my problems and she said she would help me to find a job in Holland.' According to social worker Ester Rios, such chance meetings happen frequently. 'In Greece or Cyprus these girls always meet someone in a night club who advises them to go to the Netherlands and offers to pay for her ticket.'

Maria took Viola to 'Uncle Henkie's' hotel in Rotterdam. 'Almost all the girls who worked there came from Colombia.' They had to have intercourse with their clients without condoms. If the punters complained, they got to have another go for free. 'Uncle Henkie' was a well-known criminal. At his hotel Maria introduced Viola to an Argentinian who would take care of her. Viola had to prostitute herself for him. She was rigidly controlled by a female drug-runner who was a friend of his. Viola's only confidante was a woman who worked in the same hotel, who later died, to Viola's distress.

After her friend's death, Viola had to cope with the Argentinian criminal on her own. After a while she was 'saved' by a man from the Antilles, who offered her armed protection in exchange for prostitution money. When she refused to co-operate, he pointed meaningfully at his gun. Viola realized that his armed protection might well be turned against her and eventually reported him to the police.

In the Netherlands

It is not unusual that all three women – Viola, Celestina and Hermana – were contacted in the Netherlands by profiteers who offered to deal with their difficulties as illegal immigrants in return for money. 'Those pimps know we need help,' Viola said cynically. 'They know where to pick up a girl.' Hermana said about the helpful 'friend' she met. 'He only kept me for his own relaxation. He had other girls. Problems, problems, and on top of it I got pregnant.'

Like other women in her position, Hermana abandoned her 'friend' when she discovered she could get a professional social worker for free. She wanted to go to Portugal to join her husband. But she had to take care of another problem. 'I called my husband to tell him I was pregnant. Of course he wanted to know what that was all about. I said, "All the time you were in Portugal I hardly ever heard from you. That's why I went abroad. I could only get a job in prostitution. I had an accident with a client. The condom burst." He said, "Get some help and come to Portugal as soon as you can."' Hermana was glad that he didn't react too fiercely. They are now reunited in Portugal.

The Amsterdam police wrote a report on Hermana, Celestina and Viola's experiences. 'They are interesting,' they commented, 'but we can't do anything because the traffickers are outside Holland.' However, they were able to track down their pimps. Unfortunately Viola's friend from the Antilles wasn't listed in the police files. When she was shown the photographs of well-known criminals she recognized many of her regular clients.

Celestina's pimp was known to the police, but she became frightened and withdrew her statement. He was imprisoned only to be released soon afterwards. Hermana left the Netherlands without making a statement.

9 The Belgian Billionaire gang

There were only a few customers in the night club next door to the Billionaire Club in Rotterdam the evening I went to visit it in March 1992. The majority of the girls were non-European. 'They all work here voluntarily,' the manager, who was also a dancers' agent, explained proudly. 'At my agency the women can be trained as professional dancers. I also see to their health insurance, and I never force them to do a striptease if they don't want to.' Pointing at a sturdy, shy girl sitting at the bar, he said, 'It is no good trying to make her perform a striptease. By the way, it is wellnigh impossible to employ a whole contingent of foreign strippers and prostitutes legally. Next door, at the Billionaire's, there are at least 20 foreign girls.' One of the customers interrupted us to say that a new group of Philippine women had recently arrived at the Billionaire.

In 1987 the Billionaire gang owned half of the 38 sex clubs in Rotterdam. They also ran an entertainers' agency, which they had taken over from a French couple, who had gone out of business after it became known that they had recruited 20 Thai women as 'folk dancers' and then forced them into prostitution. The Thai women had entered the Netherlands through Belgium, France and Luxemburg.

The gang had vested interests in clubs and night clubs in the Netherlands and other European countries including Denmark, Switzerland and Italy. In its heyday the gang also received the revenues from clubs in Ankara (Turkey) and the Christian part of the Lebanon,[1] and was reputed to have a branch in the United Kingdom,[2] possibly for taxation reasons. Many Dutch sex-club owners have registered their businesses as British limited companies and have an office somewhere in the United Kingdom. Taxation on such limited companies is lower than for a b.v., the Dutch equivalent.

Abroad the Billionaire gang, who were Belgian in origin, focused on various side activities. They organized drugs transportation to the United Kingdom and worked with dollar forgers. One girl was caught at the airport because she used forged dollars for her 'showmoney'. According to Dirk Trioen, a former gang member who wrote about his experiences in a book, one Belgian member called Van Engeland who fell out of favour with the gang had shipments of arms sent to Zaire on the side.[3]

The police financial bureau, popularly called the 'Strip them naked team', investigated the gang during 1991 and 1992. They confiscated the gang's books and discovered, among other things, that these Belgians had never paid any taxes and had practised false accounting. They owed over £1 million to the tax office, but rumour has it that they bought this off for only £35,000. The police found letters from customers whom they had cheated: when a customer was drunk, the waiter would get him to sign a credit-card slip twice. The managers ordered the women to steal from their customers under threat of losing their jobs.[4] The Billionaire gang are not alone in this: if all tolerated brothels in the Netherlands were checked out for these sorts of fraud, probably 50 per cent of them would have to be closed down. The Belgians also cheated the tax office by using so-called leased company cars privately on a large scale and by their takings from gambling machines. They made at least £12,000 a day but paid tax of only £1,000 a month. The Dutch tax authorities had no records for them. Their profits were deposited in accounts registered to nominal figures, but most of their money came from the prostitution racket.[5]

Rather as McDonald's runs a fast-food chain, the Belgian criminals owned a fast-sex chain. They charged large commissions for prostitutes, who were more often than not grossly underpaid, and distributed women throughout Europe. From 1987 onwards STV documented over 80 cases of women trafficked by them, so the number they dealt with must have been in the hundreds. STV's Belgian sister organization came across many women who had been smuggled to Europe with false visa stickers, stolen from the Philippine embassy. This was a speciality of gang member Freddy de Coen, who is also a former member of the right-wing political group Flemish Block.[6] From 1987 onwards the gang used the Cyprus route. At the time the police claimed not to know who was running the gang.[7]

The trafficking through Cyprus went on until 1991, when four Filipina women at last gave evidence against the gang. The women had been promised training as dancers in Cyprus, which they were given. Their careers as dancers were short-lived, however; they soon found themselves on the game in Rotterdam. The police raided the clubs belonging to the gang, but found no girls. News of the raid had leaked out and the women had been safely hidden in clubs in other cities. Later it emerged that a policeman who was not involved with the case had tipped off the gang.[8]

The case came to court in September 1991. Some information came to light but the four Filipina women who had given evidence to the police were no longer in the country and so could not be called as witnesses. The judge consequently dismissed the case and the three Belgians continued their business as usual. Two years later it was discovered that this legal catastrophe could have been averted: the women did not have to appear because their evidence had been heard at length by the examining magistrate. The public prosecutor had made a mistake, but because he was suffering from a fatal illness nobody wanted to offend him.[9]

The four Filipina women who had taken their complaints to court were the last to be trafficked by the Billionaire gang in conjunction with Ernesto B. and the investigation marked the end of the gang's Cyprus phase. The connection with the agents in Cyprus had brought them too much unwelcome publicity.

The public prosecutor was not the only person to be criticized: the Rotterdam police were too. Until 1992 they had allowed foreign women to work for three months on artists' visas. While this policy was in force, many sex-club owners suddenly started up in business as artists' agents, just as the Billionaire Club's neighbour had. Bert Bennink and Peter de Winter, two officers in the Rotterdam foreigners' police, commented, 'Through these visas we freed the women from their illegal status for three months, which allowed us to make personal contact with them. They had to report to the police station, preferably without their bosses. We could not always prevent the boss from being present, but usually we asked him to wait outside for a while. On these occasions we would register their passports and ask about any problems on the job.

'To our regret we sometimes learned from the vice squad or social workers that traffic in women had taken place under our very eyes. We might prevent these kinds of problems by putting a halt to our contacts with the bosses altogether. But then you run the risk that dozens of women will enter the country and have some man guaranteeing their living expenses and health care, which means we lose sight of them because we have to appeal to people who signed the warrant some months earlier. Now at least we know who has a contract with whom.'

The Rotterdam police were asked more than once why they didn't close down the gang's brothels; the law forbidding the exploitation of brothels was still in force and might have been useful. Their answer was that it wasn't possible to shut the clubs: those owned by the gang met the legal requirements, the residents were not restricted, the clubs were fireproof and reached the necessary standards of hygiene.

'We suspected that organized crime was taking place in these clubs, but the gang members had not been convicted of it so we couldn't ask the mayor to close them. It was a shame, because if we had been able to we would have demonstrated to the public that sex clubs can't be used to launder money. We weren't able to prove that trafficking in women was a systematic part of the brothels' management.' The police were extremely tolerant towards the clubs: when the gang opened a new one, the policeman in charge of checking clubs sent a bunch of congratulatory flowers.[10]

The fact that the gang had complied meticulously with the law was a major point in the defence at the trial and was a new element in the game of cat and mouse which the gang were playing with the police. One of the three men who ran the gang told a BBC documentary team, 'The police check the women. By the way, our contacts with the police are quite smooth. The women who work here have to decide for themselves whether they sleep with the customers or not. On their arrival all women are asked what they want to do. Sometimes they are homesick and tell their sad stories because clients like to hear them.'[11] He falsely claimed that the women left the clubs with a medical certificate stating their virginity was still intact. He also admitted to having a gun, 'just for my private collection'.

While gang members paid lip service to the regulations, they were maltreating and threatening women. One woman ended up in hospital. The gang used John David's method of torture, named after an English gangster: the violence started with the victim's fingers being broken and escalated from there, to end possibly in rape. The violence extended beyond the women victims. According to a former gang member, the threesome in Rotterdam had had one of their Belgian puppet figures, Marc Verbanck, killed by Yugoslavians.[12] Their manager in Spain was killed 'in an accident' just before he was due to take the witness stand against them.[13]

Indonesia

After the trial had been dismissed gang members decided to do their own recruiting and chose Indonesia as their new territory. One member, Jean-Paul, who hadn't been subpoenaed at the trial, was married to Ira, an Indonesian woman. Personal contacts were crucial in Indonesia because the Muslim religion forbids women to associate with strange men. Since Ira knew Indonesia well, she recruited there for the gang. She conscripted her nieces, who could easily approach their friends.

Fatima was a friend of Ira's niece. 'In Indonesia I went with my friend Mimah to a meeting about working abroad. There I met Ira and Jean-Paul. I thought Jean-Paul was very sympathetic, and even in Rotterdam I still liked him. I have always thought that he was different from the others. Ira treated us with respect too. They said I could make a lot of money working behind a bar, about £15 a day. I hadn't been in a bar before, I was a beautician in Indonesia. However, they said my lack of experience wasn't a problem and no training was required. According to Ira, women of every nationality worked in the bar and any language problems could be solved with dictionaries. I only found out later that Jean-Paul was the proprietor. I was very nervous because I didn't know what to expect. According to Ira between 15 and 20 women were needed. Eventually Ira and Jean-Paul selected eight of us. Afterwards I realized that they didn't want the fat women, but at the time I didn't notice.

'I didn't accept immediately because Europe is a long way from home. But the argument that I could give my children a better future convinced me because I was divorced. Before I left, I visited Jean-Paul a few times to arrange the details. Ira and he procured the documents. They photographed me, but not naked.' Impresarios sometimes have the women photographed naked to prevent them from maintaining afterwards they didn't know striptease was involved.

'The eight of us went to Holland on the same plane. Jean-Paul didn't travel with us. At the airport we talked to a Dutch couple, who gave us their address, and who were on the same plane. A chauffeur met us at Amsterdam airport. Since he was old and grey, we called him "daddy". On the way to Rotterdam he took away our passports. At our destination we had the shock of our lives: striptease photographs were on display in the showcases outside.

It wasn't exactly the traditional dancing for which one girl in our group had been hired.' Ill at ease, the women went inside to meet their prospective bosses.

Fatima said, 'It was very dark in the bar. I could only see dancing women. "Oh gosh," we thought, "striptease." I tried to write down the name of the bar, but one of the bosses saw me and quickly turned off the lights. We didn't dare to ask what kind of bar it was. There were some very strong and muscular men there.' Fatima giggled as she imitated their way of walking like Franken-stein's monster.

To her, one particular gang member seemed the most formidable: 'A big bold man, with a large golden chain around his neck. I can still feel his eyes on me. Nothing escaped him.' Fatima thought he was the head of the gang. Although he wasn't in fact, he was important as the head of day-to-day business.

On the first night Fatima had to watch the other strippers, 'for her own instruction'. Afterwards a man took the women to an apartment above the night club. 'A large house with many rooms, full of women. The management of the Billionaire locked the place with three keys. We could only peer at the outside world through a window. They didn't feed us and the other women living there had hardly anything either, but kindly gave us one bowl of noodle soup and an egg to share between the four of us. Most of them came from Latin American countries and the Philippines. We couldn't understand them, but we gathered that they had not been paid one penny so far.'

On their third day in the Netherlands the Indonesian women had to wait more than an hour in the artists' agency's office. Meanwhile Ira telephoned from Jakarta. According to Fatima, she had problems obtaining passports. After the call, Jean-Paul said he had to go to Jakarta with another gang member to take care of urgent business. 'And you lot are leaving soon for Belgium,' he told the four Indonesian women, to their surprise.

In Belgium they were taken to a bar in Ghent. Again they were housed in an apartment above the bar. Fatima said, 'We had to work for different people there. We were only supposed to drink with the guests and usually they didn't stay with me for long because they couldn't understand me. The bartender told them that I was shy because I was new. He told me that a drink might relax me, provided I didn't get drunk. For the first time in my life I had an alcoholic drink. I am a Muslim, you see, and Muslims don't drink alcohol.

'The next day we went to the place where we were eventually going to work, where we had to stage a striptease act. My friend Mimah, who spoke some English, translated the manager's instructions. We said that we could not possibly dance naked the next evening – "No problem," we would learn. Playing for time, we objected that we didn't have suitable clothes. But they were prepared for that. That was not all. We *might* have sex with customers. Imagine – we didn't *have* to, we were allowed to. The bar had "séparés" for the purpose, little private rooms for sexual intercourse with customers. These men meant business and time was running out. We plotted to call the couple we had met at the airport. In the morning we said that we had to do some shopping. The bartenders were still drunk from the night before and let us go. They didn't even notice that we were hardly dressed. We had already been given our passports back. I never understood why. Other women had to go without passports for months on end. The men had told the Filipina women that the police needed their passports all that time.'

The four women walked barefoot through the Belgian town, looking for the Dutch village Krimpen aan de Lek, where the Dutch couple lived. Of course no one in Ghent knew where it was. The women finally managed to phone the couple with the help of assistants at an Indonesian food shop, a toko. The Dutch couple came as soon as they could and took them to report to the police; in vain, as it later turned out. Fatima then lived with the couple for some time.

From the gang's point of view, Fatima and her friends were failures. The gang members didn't succeed in forcing them into prostitution. 'Thanks be to Allah, because we refused to do that immoral work,' Fatima said to me. Ira, who had worked in Indonesia for the gang, had not selected the most 'suitable' submissive Indonesian women. After Fatima and the other girls escaped, Ira was thrown out of the gang. Her associates got away with it. Since the gang had not been able to force the women into prostitution, Fatima's complaint to the police failed. The police could only bring a prosecution if the women had been forced to have sexual intercourse with the customers.

The police said about their stay in the Netherlands, 'Nothing really happened. All right, they were locked up, but that's not sufficient proof to convict of trafficking. Nor were they beaten up.' And they said about the women's short trip to Belgium: 'That happened in Belgium and not in the Netherlands. In Belgium they didn't use force when the women refused to strip. And the women were not explicitly told to have sex with customers. They could only infer that from the context.'

Fatima was indignant: 'I loathe the idea of being in a séparé with a customer. Jean-Paul and the others should be locked away. It makes me sad to think of that week. I am penniless and I lost my job in Indonesia.' However, the gang were warned that the police were still monitoring their activities. Besides, the journalist Chris de Stoop was about to publish his book in Belgium on the gang's time in Cyprus; a further reason for them to be more careful. Nevertheless, they had plenty of time to prepare for their next venture.

Poland

'Sometimes the girls from the Billionaire Club come in here crying,' the manager of the next-door club said to me. 'I help them and take them to a hotel. And then what happens? The police can't find the time to investigate the complaints against the gang.'

A few weeks after our conversation, some Polish women turned up on the manager's doorstep, one of whom was Kasha aged 22. According to Kasha, six girls were brought by bus from Poland every week. Some 500 women from all over Poland had been transported to western European countries. The women had been recruited by a new member of the Billionaire gang, a man called Lech, who was a former schoolteacher. In Poland he managed an employment agency for the gang.

Kasha told me her story. 'I saw an advertisement in a regional Polish newspaper for waitresses and receptionists. No knowledge of English was required, which seemed an advantage. I hesitated a long time before answering, but eventually I wrote. The company sent me a lot of information, which I sent back with a note to say that I wasn't interested. But the agency kept sending me glossy brochures, with promises of employment in Belgium and the Netherlands. I thought, "The Netherlands are beautiful." I talked it over at length with my mother. I lived with my parents and got on well with them; we badly needed the salary they were offering. My mother wasn't working, which is unusual in Poland. She looked after my brother, who is an invalid. My father had a job. My mother thought I ought to go, but she was afraid that something was wrong. But, after a few weeks I decided to go for it. The fact that I wasn't happy at the butcher's where I worked tipped the balance. Besides, I only had to go to the Netherlands for three months. "I can manage that," I thought.

'The brochures contained a telephone number. I thought a call could do no harm. The company was too far away to visit easily. This man Lech answered. He said we were to leave within a couple of days, which was too soon for my liking. That wasn't a problem; he said I could join the group which was leaving a week later.

'I agreed and packed my belongings. My mother decided to see me off and we took the night train to the town where the agency was. We phoned the office from the station and they said they would come to collect us. We waited for over an hour in the cold.' Kasha burst out laughing. 'I had seen a very small ramshackle vehicle, but I didn't think it was their car. My mother and I took no notice of it. And of course they hadn't bargained on there being two of us.'

After another phone call, mother and daughter finally found the agency's office. 'We sat there without anyone paying attention to us. The staff were too busy picking up other girls. Eventually we went down town because we had some time on our hands. Before we left for the Netherlands, they took my mother to the station.'

Kasha travelled by bus with six other girls. 'Lech drove us. We had to share two blankets between us, and it was terribly cold. Two girls quit in Rotterdam. One of them decided to visit her family on the spur of the moment, and the other took the next bus back to Poland because she didn't like what was going on. I had second thoughts too, but I decided to go on because otherwise I would have gone to a lot of trouble for nothing. And after all we were supposed to be working in an ordinary office.'

That night Kasha stayed in a hotel. The next day she and her travel companions were taken to an apartment above the night club which she described as 'terribly dirty'. The following morning the girls had to go into the office one by one and introduce themselves. The men inside were talking and hardly took any notice of Kasha. Casually they made it clear that she had to undress. Kasha said, 'I wondered what that was supposed to mean. Was I to have a medical check-up? I thought maybe they wanted to see if I washed regularly.' The men never bothered to talk in a language which Kasha spoke, but they did give her a contract in strange English which stated: 'This contract is valid for three months. The artist will receive a standard £10 a day. Additionally the artist will cash £15 a day for performances.' It also said that, among other bonuses, Kasha would receive 10 per cent of the profits on the champagne consumed by clients she had a drink with.

The artists' agency was contractually obliged to pay the girls' return fares to Poland; it was also supposed to arrange housing, work permits and pay any taxes. In return, the artist had to declare she was healthy and not pregnant, and have a medical check up. She could be fined £150 in the following instances: if she broke her contract and left within three months; if she left the club in working hours; and if she was absent from the job.

Kasha was astonished when she gathered from the contract that she was not going to be a receptionist but an 'artist'. Later she discovered that this meant striptease and prostitution. Kasha said, 'I only realized when we were ushered into the club. A Polish woman who had been working there for some time tried to encourage us. "It's not as bad as it seems," she said. However, we soon found out that she was the new girlfriend of one of the bosses. Lech had already befriended the girls who arrived before us, so they were no help.

'By the absurd terms of the contract we had to dance naked. The first day we only had to watch to learn the trade. We wanted to tell the boss that we had never agreed to striptease, but instead of taking our complaints seriously, he said that we would only get our money after we had had sex with customers. And if we didn't, we wouldn't receive our commission for the champagne.'

The Polish women were never beaten up by the gang; one look at the men was enough to make the girls obey them. Kasha remembered especially the frightening eyes of her boss. She didn't know of his reputation for violence. She had only heard that in Belgium he had women working for him behind the windows. The gang used being sent to Belgium as a threat: they said it meant earning no money at all.

Eventually the girls were paid a sum which an ordinary working girl in Holland would never accept. And, of course, they couldn't refuse clients, which is a 'fundamental' prostitute's right.

Kasha stood it for no more than two months. One night she and some colleagues passed the night club next door to the Billionaire. They started talking to the doorman and complained about their wages. He had heard these stories before and introduced them to the manager, who offered them jobs with better conditions.

They accepted and then were paid the usual fees for sleeping with punters. This time Kasha was allowed to refuse clients. After a few weeks Kasha's mother came to visit her in the Netherlands. She was told that Kasha only had to drink champagne with her customers, which was not true.

One Polish girl in Kasha's group had asked the agency before she left Poland whether she would have to work as a prostitute. 'Absolutely not, prostitution is forbidden in the Netherlands,' Lech had said. 'Dutchmen are different from Polish people, they are satisfied when you look at them with your beautiful eyes.' Another girl's contract stated that she would never have sexual contact with the club's customers.

Social workers in Rotterdam advised Kasha and her friends to report the Belgians to the police. The police gave them three months to consider lodging a complaint, although they wanted to make statements immediately. It then became clear that it was the police, not the women who needed time. They were reluctant to pursue the case: some of them believed the women were merely involved in a labour dispute in a semi-legal setting and that failure to keep the terms of contracts and poor pay were insufficient reasons to charge the gang. The police had a further problem: 'We can't prove that the Billionaire gang instructed a Polish contact person to offer the women jobs as waitresses or as receptionists. We can't definitely pinpoint the organization in the Netherlands. The Polish women were neither imprisoned nor beaten up. Their passports were not confiscated and after all they had a contract. It is true they were underpaid. But we can hardly prove they were manipulated into prostitution. We can't check it in Poland, relations with the Polish police are not that good.'

In June 1994 some members of the Polish police visited their colleagues in Rotterdam to trade information about trafficking. At their meeting Policewoman Wieslawa Sztylkowska of the Polish General Police Headquarters asked questions about this particular case: 'In Poland we arrested four traffickers of the Billionaire. The Polish state attorney had assumed that the managers of the club would also be brought to trial in the Netherlands. But that never happened.'[14]

One of the Dutch police replied, 'We would welcome a Polish police rogatory commission to the Netherlands. We have given the Polish police a lot of information. It is thanks to the Polish women who complained to us that the traffickers were arrested in Poland.'

Afterwards Wieslawa, who is in charge of all the cases of trafficking in Poland, said, 'They missed the opportunity of a lifetime. They could have talked seriously with me. Probably they didn't realize how high my rank is in the Polish police.' She was speechless when she heard of the Rotterdam police's reluctance to take statements from the Polish women who had worked in the Billionaire Club in 1992.

Disintegration of the Billionaire gang

In August 1993 there were still reports of women shouting for help from the Billionaire's windows. At the time the place was packed with Hungarian and Czech girls. The night club's new choreographer wanted to leave but didn't dare. According to some sources the girls were filled up with vitamin pills to keep them going. Business was slack: too many journalists had invaded the place, chasing the punters away.[15] The tax office was also on to them, so they decided to set up in Spain. At the time the gang was cracking up. One of the first gang members to quit was an international footballer who had the expertise to set up on his own.[16] Long before the fall of the Berlin Wall, he had been running an agency in Budapest which sent women to Austria and Italy. Even under the communists Budapest was the best place for eastern European traffickers, and Arab tourists had always visited the city. From Budapest women go to Luxemburg and Scandinavian countries.

Between 1975 and 1985 the gang's impresario was V., who used to engage famous pop groups to perform in Belgium.[17] He also quit the gang. Another dissident gang member, Dirk Trioen, was threatened because he had taken pity on a few girls. He pretended they had run away and moved them elsewhere to work on more favourable terms. He was the manager of the bar where the Indonesian girls were housed. He had a knack of organizing cartels and smuggling and he knew how to handle corrupt Belgian policemen. He was also active in EC fraud.

One Filapina was rescued by the gang's former chauffeur, who had to break away from the Billionaire because he fell in love with her and asked her to marry him after he had divorced his first wife. Because he feared reprisals by the gang, he demanded help and financial support from the Dutch authorities. When he didn't get it soon enough, he threatened to disclose the whereabouts of the shelter where he and his fiancée were hiding out. He is now divorced from his first wife and the Filipina has a residence permit in Belgium.

However, it was not until 1994 that two bosses of the Billionaire gang were finally arrested, at the end of what had been a shameful chapter for both Belgium and the Netherlands.

10 'I'll be safer in Yugoslavia than in the Netherlands'

Former Yugoslavia has been both a sending and a target country. Because of the war and its specific economic and social conditions, the new Balkan states are becoming increasingly involved in worldwide sex trafficking. As with a real crossroads, they are currently at the intersection of many trafficking routes. Young women accept 'tempting' jobs in Greece, Cyprus, Italy, Germany, France, Sweden and so on. From Belgrade many go west, and some others go to the Middle East to work as dancers. Others have not returned home. Zarita, who comes from Serbia, talked to me just after she had gone to the police. 'In Yugoslavia we hear very little about criminal gangs abroad,' she said. 'My ex-husband, who had worked in Germany, once told me that Yugoslavian prostitutes have a hard time in the Netherlands and Germany and that few girls leave prostitution alive and well.'

As a girl, Zarita had taken up ju-jitsu because she wanted to be a policewoman. She hadn't achieved her ambition because her family did not have enough money for her education, but her training meant she wasn't afraid of reprisals. In Serbia she had had to make do with a job in a factory. She told me, 'I made about £30 a month. I changed my job to work as a waitress in Holland. I was to earn £1,250–£1,750 per month in an all-night restaurant and my 16-year-old niece was to come with me as a dishwasher. We saw the jobs in a magazine called *Advertisements*. It gave a Belgrade telephone number, which I rang. The phone was answered by Bata, who is the man I have just reported to the police. He explained the job's conditions and I decided to accept it. We arranged to meet at a bus stop, where he picked my niece and me up and took us to the house of a friend of his in Belgrade. Two other girls also going to the Netherlands were there. I didn't find any of this strange because I had found a job in a restaurant in

Germany before in a similar way. That first time I really worked as a waitress and stayed with a nice family.'

Other women were less fortunate in their first attempts to find employment in western Europe. Yasmin, who is a former Yugoslavian and now tries to help her fellow countrywomen, said, 'Usually the traffickers promise girls a job as a waitress.' From her career as a voluntary social worker, Yasmin has a vast body of knowledge of criminal networks in former Yugoslavia. 'These traffickers often promise the women work in restaurants. They even mention the restaurant by name to make the enterprise look trustworthy and so that the women's families can keep in touch with them. When parents phone, they are told, "So and so is out for a few minutes, but she'll call you back." Eventually she calls, with a gun pointed at her head. She is made to say cheerfully how well she is doing. The restaurant owner usually doesn't know what is going on, but thinks he is doing a regular customer a favour,' explained Yasmin.

Zarita took up her story again. 'Bata, which was his nickname, promised to take us from Belgrade to The Hague in Holland. After he had dropped us, he was going on to Belgium. I was glad that we were going straight to the Netherlands by car. I even offered him 300 German marks for petrol, which wasn't much considering that a train ticket is more expensive. Just before our departure I wanted to give him the marks, but he said, "Pay later, when you have earned enough money."

'A Bulgarian girl joined us. I was told later that she was travelling on a borrowed Yugoslavian passport, which Bata sent back after we reached Holland. Her own identity papers, which were only valid in Yugoslavia, were taken away from her.

'Bata's brother-in-law and his girlfriend, who helped Bata force women into prostitution, were to accompany us to Germany. Later it emerged that Bata could not travel through Germany because he was wanted by the German police.'

For Zarita the journey to Holland went without a hitch. 'When we arrived we stayed with a friend of Bata's. Nothing happened. After a few days I wanted to see the restaurant where we were supposed to be working. At first Bata said that the proprietor wasn't ready to receive us yet. Next he said we might not be able to work in the restaurant after all.'

When they heard this, the women wondered if they had really been taken on to work as waitresses. The Bulgarian woman thought that a co-operative attitude might help, and said that she was willing to accept other work, cleaning for instance. Bata seemed pleased, although of course he did have another job in mind: behind a prostitution window.

When Bata finally told the women this, he locked them up and confiscated their personal belongings. He didn't allow them to make any more phone calls. In the meantime his friends were persuading them to give in. The brother-in-law's girlfriend worked on the Bulgarian woman, but she wasn't successful. The woman became upset and withdrawn. 'Don't make a fool of yourself. You already sold yourself in Belgrade,' she was told.

Zarita's niece nagged her, 'Let's do it just for a couple of months, no one will ever know.' Her niece had become co-operative because she was having an affair with Bata and was pregnant by him. 'These men promise the women the world. Sometimes they use their own girlfriends to draw unwilling women across the line,' Yasmin told me. Apparently the niece had taken it upon herself to persuade Zarita. 'I could tell from the blood on the sheets that he had deflowered her, but he certainly did not rape her,' Zarita said. 'I got irritated with Bata's bragging about his affair with my niece. I felt cheated, because at first she had told me there was nothing between them. She didn't tell me he had promised to marry her. To make matters worse, he never told my niece he was already married.'

This love did not last. Zarita said, 'Bata paid a man £300 to find a brothel where my niece and I could work. This man had a relative who owned a sex club in The Hague. So for him it was a piece of cake to earn £300. I considered my niece too young for that kind of work. On top of that I thought it ridiculous that this person got his £300 while we were paid nothing at all. Once a week Bata collected our money from the boss. After three weeks I said I needed my share to go back to Yugoslavia. The owner of the club said he would have to discuss it first with Bata. I told him that Bata had nothing to do with it. This conversation was in Russian, which the boss, although he was Dutch, could understand. Of course, we were never paid a single penny.' The niece soon went off by herself to work in a brothel, which she was taken from by the police. Bata was shocked on hearing this. 'A girl who carried his baby could not be a common prostitute,' Zarita said, although it was Bata who had set her up in prostitution in the first place.

'I kept hoping that Bata would give me my money, so that I could go home. He often promised me that I would have it as soon as other people had paid their debts to him. It turned out afterwards that he had borrowed money himself from a well-known

Yugoslavian bankrobber.' By then Zarita had realized that she would never be paid.

The sex-club owner who had leased the two women wasn't happy with Zarita, who was too rebellious, and asked Bata to find her work elsewhere. This wasn't a problem: Bata's contacts could put Zarita behind the windows and she started there soon after. Zarita wasn't very talkative about her work as a prostitute. She would only say, 'I disliked everything, and I mean everything, about it. Besides, I made very little money.'

When Zarita was working the windows, Bata would constantly check on her by phone. Zarita discovered that he worked with Turkish and Moroccan criminals: his brother-in-law warned her that she would be sold to a Moroccan if she continued to be a nuisance. Bata had already approached a Moroccan who was willing to pay £1,500 for her. When this prospective buyer arrived to inspect his merchandise, Zarita hit him with an ashtray. The Moroccan backed out of the deal. 'Too dangerous,' he told Bata afterwards. At a later point Bata tried to sell her to a second Moroccan, who was disabled. This sale also failed because by then Zarita had reported Bata to the police.

Zarita said, 'Just think of it, they simply sell you. I got goose pimples when I heard that this Moroccan would feed me so many drugs that I wouldn't be able to recognize my own child. I have no idea what drugs he was referring to.' At this point Yasmin added that many former Yugoslavian prostitutes in the Netherlands are transferred to Moroccan pimps.

Not long afterwards Zarita went to Vienna on Bata's orders with his brother-in-law. During the trip Zarita began to realize how well connected Bata was. Before they left, Bata had told Zarita with a grin that they were to collect a new girl, who thought she was going to work as a seamstress. Zarita had to go with the brother-in-law to inspire trust in the girl. The brother-in-law told Zarita that this was not the first time he had had to collect Bata's girls. Bata had tried to force a French girl into prostitution. He had learned French during a stay in France, which had been useful for trafficking French girls. However this girl owned a gun, which she fired at Bata before running off.

According to Yasmin, Vienna is an important transit point for rackets in former Yugoslavia. From here girls are taken to clubs with restricted admittance in Hamburg and other German cities.[1]

During the trip to Vienna Zarita questioned the brother-in-law. 'I wanted to learn more about Bata's group so I could tell the police later on. But first I wanted to find out if there was any point in reporting to the police.' Zarita discovered that Bata had brought a man called Milos to the Netherlands to burgle houses for him. 'Milos was a dangerous man. He had eliminated a man nicknamed Pitbull and was reputed to be a rapist. He was arrested by the police, but the foreigners' police took over and let him go.' Zarita had every reason to be afraid of Milos, who had once called her to threaten her. 'I'll make a salad of your child,' he had said. Zarita was too frightened to tell the police this.

'I also heard that Bata and his friends had stolen crates containing weapons. In all Bata had spent seven years in prison. His group consisted of about 30 people. The police were looking for them in Belgium, France and Germany. Later on I visited a Yugoslavian club with the police and there were quite a few gangsters. They are supposedly well connected at embassies.'

After hesitating, Zarita went on, 'If I told you all the details, you would be in danger yourself. But I know who killed who and who is being looked for by the police.'

Zarita described Bata as a minor criminal, who would sooner or later be thrown out by the gang. Yasmin agreed: 'His bragging and boasting could have incited someone to shoot him. Besides, he was not qualified for traffic in women. He was no great organizer.' His brother-in-law thought that he was careless, which is possibly why he told Zarita so much, thereby estranging himself from Bata.

It was during the trip to Vienna that Zarita decided to go to the police. She already knew too much and her life was in danger. She met a Yugoslavian punter, who allowed her to hide at his home. Zarita said, 'But the gang soon found me. Bata telephoned my new friend and said that he was going to tell the police that this boy was my new pimp. Bata and his friends also tried to blackmail me with photographs of me behind the window.' She laughed as she added that she had been smart enough to take the films. 'They never expected that.'

In the Netherlands Zarita could only find work as a prostitute. The boy she was living with tried to find her a job in a regular Yugoslavian bar. But the bars were all well staffed with refugees from former Yugoslavia. Zarita saw no other option to working the windows again. One day two Yugoslavs whom she knew to be important came by her window. They said, 'We know you have talked to the police. We'll follow you wherever you go.' 'Mind your own business,' Zarita answered. 'That did not stop them. On the day I filed my complaint with the police, a few of them were hanging around the police station.'

Bata made a last clumsy attempt to revenge himself on Zarita. He phoned her to say he had told her family that she had run away with stolen money. But nobody believed him.

After she had seen the police, Zarita was anxious to return to former Yugoslavia, but she had to stay in the Netherlands for a few weeks for medical treatment. She was suffering from internal bleeding after being kicked by Bata. 'When I'm back in Yugoslavia, I am going to write a book about these gangs myself,' Zarita announced. 'My family is going to move so I can live with my parents again. The gang won't be able to find me. I'll be safer in Yugoslavia than in the Netherlands. These criminals can never enter Yugoslavia. If Bata comes back, he will be sentenced to another ten years in prison,' she said optimistically.

Several weeks after Zarita's departure, the Bulgarian woman also denounced Bata and his friends to the police, who had removed her from a shelter for refugees. The statements of the two women led to a police investigation and a court case. At the trial, in August 1992, the Bulgarian woman testified against Bata, although she was terrified because he had threatened her. Afterwards she said she had found it difficult because she had had to relive her experiences. 'I wished I would never have to think about it again. But that's impossible. I'll never forget it as long as I live.'

Bata was sentenced to two years' imprisonment in his absence. The Bulgarian woman said, 'Two years, 20 years, it will never be enough for what he did to me and the others.' The brother-in-law got off scot-free because he had been a witness for the prosecution. The police were present in court in force. Policeman Nico van der Geest said, 'If Bata had appeared we would have taken him in immediately. Unfortunately after Zarita filed her complaint, we had to let him go. Next the Bulgarian woman turned up with fresh evidence. But we had no proof of his international connections. We only knew that he was *persona non grata* in Germany. Still, we have always considered this a real case of traffic in women. Such a pity that it only resulted in his conviction in his absence.'

The police and the Bulgarian woman left the court house disappointed. It is true that a relatively small-time criminal, Bata, had been convicted, but he had to be caught first. The other members of the network had escaped unharmed. In 1994 Bata finally did go to prison. According to Yasmin, one of his associates was found dead in an Amsterdam canal.

Also in 1994 there was another victim of a gang from former Yugoslavia who preferred to return to Bosnia to get away from her traffickers. She had gone to the Netherlands, where acquaintances of hers already lived, to escape from the war. She couldn't find a job, but met some friendly people who invited her to stay with them because she was a refugee. As she didn't want to outstay her welcome, she went to live with a friend of a friend. This woman gave her a fatal introduction to her brother, who, with help from another man, made her go on the game. The woman's brother took her to a cheap hotel, locked her up and threatened her: 'Whore, I'll kill you if you don't obey.' He extorted £16,000 from her.

At the subsequent trial he denied everything. He said in his own defence, 'I was involved in a relationship with her. She asked me to rent a window for her. She was down and out. She had spent all her money on drugs and in the discothèque. A Dutch boy found a prostitution room for her. I disagreed with her working in prostitution. They may say my friends and I brandished firearms. I didn't and I don't know how my friends got them. If my friends have said that the girl was afraid of me, they only said it because they were jealous. I made contradictory statements because the war had made me confused.' He denied being in the hotel where the girl was kept under lock and key, but this was refuted by other witnesses and the two young men were found guilty. All the cases and even the statements about Balkan syndicates have the depressing ingredients of personal resentment and violence.

Escalation in traffic from former Yugoslavia

STV began to notice an increase in trafficked women from Yugoslavia from 1988 onwards. Up till the present time, women haven't played a major part in these groups, which is possibly why rape and macho behaviour are rampant. Yugoslav crooks terrorize both female and male prostitutes. A rent boy said, 'I avoid Yugoslavian clients for my own safety. They'll do anything for next to nothing.' Dutch criminals are also afraid of those from former Yugoslavia.

In trafficking cases there is a sharp division of labour in Yugoslavian gangs: one section recruits the girls, a second collects them and a third guards them. Sometimes the guardians may enter into friendly relationships with the girls. Male procurers, who operate in the background, are more prestigious than the ordinary working pimps, who stand out because of their vulgar behaviour. 'Bata was such a hard-working, vulgar pimp,' Yasmin said.

Relationships between group members are strictly regulated according to certain codes. Yasmin again: 'It is not done to treat women exceedingly badly, for instance by giving them no money at all. In that case women have nothing to lose. Women without money will walk out and go to the police. So to keep the women quiet, the traffickers sometimes give them small sums of money. That's why Bata sent Zarita's father enough money to buy a cow. It also quietened any suspicions Zarita's father might have.'

Yugoslavian criminals were always free to travel to the west and settled in western Europe long before the Berlin Wall came down. After 1989 they could profit more easily from their knowledge of Slavonic languages, which enabled them to contact women in several eastern European countries, like the Bulgarian woman who was Zarita's partner in misfortune.

There have been many more women since Zarita, for instance one Russian woman was promised a job in Belgrade but was exploited in prostitution by a Bosnian recruiter. A young girl who was trafficked by a Bosnian was forced to invite her sister. She then disappeared into thin air, so we'll never know if she had come to terms with feelings of guilt she expressed after her release. A Croatian man lured women into prostitution from former Yugoslavia and Austria. Several Yugoslavian girls had to work in prostitution with a gun pointed at their heads. One of them was driven alongside an Amsterdam canal. 'Do what I say, or otherwise you'll be drowned,' her 'special protector' told her. The gang also used the old weapon of threatening the family at home. They even managed to recruit a Polish girl who was looking at a bulletin board at the orthodox church in Vienna.

According to the police, the gang was a large one with about 200 members,[2] although the women had only counted 40 or so. They didn't know all of them, but were terrified when two of the gang were murdered. One had fled from Sarajevo because he had killed a policeman, and his body was later found cut in pieces in a rubbish bag. The gang also dealt in arms, drugs, gambling, murder and kidnapping. When police raided one of their gambling dens, a policeman was shot and seriously wounded. The gang had no political background and all the different Yugoslavian nationalities worked together. For them the civil war didn't matter, except in one respect: it made it easier to recruit women.

Not all gangs are politically neutral. 'Some ex-Yugoslavians in western Europe, who are dabbling in arms smuggling, drug traffic and the prostitution racket, are financing the unruly militias waging war in former Yugoslavia. Those gangs don't necessarily have to ship the weapons themselves. In Germany there is a group which wants to realize the goal of a Greater Serbia,' Yasmin said.

In the Netherlands the Criminal Intelligence Unit suspects, but has no proof, that the war is being financed by the profits from drugs and other crimes.

Picking up the pieces

In former Yugoslavia women's groups are having to cope with the effects of the war, including wartime prostitution. One of these organizations is the SOS Hotline in Belgrade, where Violetta Krasnic, a psychologist, and Zorica Mrsevic, a criminologist, both work. They said, 'Since the war the number of calls to the hotline has increased by 30 per cent. The violence the women report is becoming heavier. Due to the war men have more weapons, and are now experienced killers and experts on torture. One man told his terrified wife, "I could kill anyone, I am a criminal." Women who have fought in the war also have problems; sometimes they go out at the weekend to kill people.

'Though it is formally forbidden, trafficking in women is a crime with little risk attached. Organized criminals are increasingly involved in pimping in our own country. They don't only control the traditional areas, but also recent developments like escort agencies: last year more than 100 new agencies advertised in local papers, all run by criminal organizations. You only have to call them once and that is the end of your freedom. We know of one girl who went to see what it was like. The management stopped her leaving. She only escaped by pretending she had a sexually transmitted disease.

'Many gypsies also call our hotline. Some gypsy families are involved in trafficking. Albanian girls are sold by people from their own community through two channels. Since 1991 at least 70 Albanian women have been trafficked inside Kosovo and from Albania to Yugoslavia and other countries. During the last decade Yugoslavia has been a target country for traffickers from eastern Europe. As far as we know the first group of trafficked women were Ukrainians who thought they were going to work in restaurants.

When they were naïve enough to come to the west, they had to entertain lorry drivers.

'Now we are dealing with refugee women, who are abused in the war zones. We have heard that in Serbia Bosnian women are trafficked when they arrive in the refugee centres. There are special networks, based in Kiev in Russia, which procure women for the soldiers at Unprofor [United Nations protection force] headquarters in Croatia. In the brothels there are also women captured from "the other side".

'Another problem is the trade embargo and the opportunities it offers organized crime to control the situation. Oil is smuggled by the Yugoslav mafia and other eastern European gangs. For oil smuggling you need a high level of corruption, otherwise it is too difficult. It's controlled by war veterans, who will never be satisfied with the status quo. When the embargo is lifted, Yugoslav organized crime will spread throughout Europe.'

11 The red mafia

'The police in the city of Leeuwarden have rounded up 16 illegal women and men, mostly of eastern European origin,' Dutch radio reported in its early morning news on 11 February 1994. The arrests were the start of an investigation into a case which was typical of the criminal activities of eastern European gangs. Some of the women apprehended had been recruited in Russia by an organization which promised them a glamorous life as dancers. A few of them produced expired visas; one worked at a travel agency, which sold the visas the gang trafficking the women had obtained from the embassy. It is common practice for travel agencies in eastern European countries to sell visas. Two of the women had offers of work from a company, which proved to be forgeries. The other women had all been promised careers as high-class call girls.[1] All the women were trapped by debt; they had been tricked by different traffickers, but had all been taken to the same town, Leeuwarden, where the brothel-owner kept track of their debts, while conning them out of a lot more money. They were subjected to the classic controls of traffickers, such as handing over their passports and money. There was a camera in every room, so escape was impossible. The gang had intimidated them by threatening to sell them: they were even introduced to their prospective buyers, which terrified them all. 'I worked voluntarily because if I hadn't things would have been even worse,' one of the women said when she was told that there is a law against traffic in women. She said she didn't mind being exploited, she came from Russia where women are used to it. She clearly didn't want to take the matter any further.

The appearance on the scene of criminals and traffickers from eastern and central Europe, the so-called red mafia, caused great changes in the trade in women. After the fall of the Berlin Wall the numbers of women trafficked from eastern Europe increased dramatically. Now almost 80 per cent of STV's clients are from central and eastern European countries, whereas before 1989 they were only 1 or 2 per cent. Polish and Czech women usually travel overland, which is cheaper than flying. They come by car or minibus, and sometimes on package tours on which they are told by the traffickers to get off the bus in Germany. The women then meet their traffickers at taxi ranks, petrol stations or parking lots.

Russian women usually travel by air, sometimes on a Polish passport. As yet Poles don't need visas to enter the Netherlands, whereas Russians do. The women are usually told just as they are boarding the plane that they have to carry a Polish passport. This intimidates them since they were not always aware of it beforehand. The traffickers use the women's anxiety to enforce their own terms: they send the women to countries other than those they thought they were going to and instruct them what to tell the authorities. For example, one woman said that none of the characteristics of trafficking applied to her. Another said at once before she was questioned, 'No, I have come of my own accord, I have kept my own passport and my money.' Apparently she had arrived at a brothel in a godforsaken village after a long taxi ride. She signalled to the group's spokeswoman to show that she hadn't given anything away. After a long time she said finally that she hadn't been taken in an ordinary taxi and that someone had promised to marry her if she kept her mouth shut.

The women are reluctant to talk because eastern European gangs are extremely violent and use every kind of threat to intimidate them. Since the red mafia arrived on the scene, killings to maintain the balance of power between traffickers have increased. They are said to have made a woman dig her own grave,[2] and they have kidnapped prostitutes simply to settle a dispute,[3] and not only prostitutes. For example, one woman at the police station seemed very upset but persisted in stating that she had not been wronged. She just wanted to be deported as soon as possible. It later emerged that her child had been taken hostage in Russia and she had decided to go back to negotiate with the traffickers. Another Russian woman saw on television the picture of a girl who had arrived in the same group as her. The girl was dead and her photograph was being shown as part of an appeal by the police for information. Eastern European criminals don't restrict themselves to trafficking, but usually sell arms and drugs on the side, which makes them even more dangerous.

Some eastern European brokers have promised women political asylum, to which they are not usually entitled. Another relatively new trick is to give women false job offers from existing companies. In November 1994 one group was convicted of practising this trick. One of its members was a Dutchman, Jan W., a former naval officer who is now a brothel-owner. He boasted that he had excellent contacts in Russia. He and his associates were also said to deal in uranium, which he denied. He was a prominent member of the VER, the Dutch Association of Relaxhouses, from which he is now probably barred. In an interview in the VER magazine he denied all the charges pending against him. 'My only mistake was that I had a few illegal Russian women working for me,' he said, and compared to the Russian-Dutch couple he worked with he seemed a minor crook. The husband is a Dutch ex-teacher who ran a computer company. His Russian wife ran an 'artists' agency' in Kiev with her mother, which took care of recruitment. The couple falsified the company's business correspondence to get Russian women into the Netherlands. The letterheads of innocent business associates were cut off original letters and pasted on to false job offers, which were then faxed to the Dutch embassy to obtain visas for the women. The six women they had recruited were unaware of all this: they thought they were going to work in the entertainment industry.

One of their victims was promised a job as a waitress in a lonely hearts club. She had been told explicitly that she wouldn't have to work as a prostitute, but when she arrived this was not the case. She protested on several occasions, but to no avail. She even had to work when she was menstruating. The other girl, H., who filed charges, was also promised a career in entertainment. 'A man approached me on the streets of Kiev and asked me if I wanted to join a ballet show. I gave him my telephone number. For a long time I heard no more. Suddenly I learned that impresarios from the Netherlands and Denmark had arrived and would hire me as an erotic dancer. I was promised that my family would never find out. The worst thing I would have to do was strip, but they said they could probably find me some other employment.'[4] Her mother advanced her the money for the ticket. Again she had to wait a long time and spent the money she had borrowed on other things. When the time finally arrived for her to go, she had to borrow more money.

A contact of the gang's took her via Budapest to the Netherlands. H. said, 'In my broken English I told the managing director of the computing company that I didn't want to go into prostitution, but from his expression I realized that he was taking no notice of me.' So prostitution it was for a couple of months.

H. was pressured to pay her debts at an interest rate of 20 per cent and some sturdy men were meant to be on their way to enforce this. Before they arrived, H. was deported by the police. She went home, but didn't dare to tell her husband that she had had to have sex with the customers. Shortly afterwards she received a fax from the Netherlands instructing her to return. She was too frightened to refuse and so back she went. In the Netherlands she managed to start a relationship with a client from the brothel, who paid her release money, and went to live with him at an address unknown to the gang. One of the gang wrote a worried letter to the police in her husband's name to find out her address. In the meantime her husband in Kiev was being harassed by gang members and decided to leave. He joined her at the client's house and pretended to be her brother.

Although the women trafficked by the gang had received a number of threatening phone calls, they did not retract their statements. The couple, who were accused of threatening them with their contacts in the Russian mafia, denied the charges strenuously. 'I just wanted to protect the women from the mafia,' one of them said. The female suspect, who was 26 and a wisp of a girl, said she felt like a victim herself, and then came up with the classic excuse that she only wanted to help the women. However, it emerged from police telephone taps that the traffickers had called their assistants to enlist witnesses for the defence. They were each sentenced to a year's imprisonment. At the trial Jan W., the brothel-owner, confessed to having confiscated the women's earnings. He also admitted possessing weapons and drugs illegally. He was found guilty of being an accomplice to trafficking and was sentenced for that and two other offences he had also confessed to.

In another big case with a similar background women had been invited to the Netherlands by a group who did above-board business as well as 'irregular' trade. Of all things, the women were supposed to sell tulips in Amsterdam, a scam organized by two Russian police officers. The women were given official invitations stamped by the Dutch authorities. Two of the women went to live with clients, but the gang tracked them down and made the men pay.[5]

Recruitment via asylum

Two Romanian women were swimming a river from Poland to Germany. Their luggage was on land in a car. They had been recruited by a Romanian woman, Veronica P., who was meant to hand them over to a Turkish organization in Germany. The swimming women knew something was wrong, but where could they go? They were in the middle of nowhere and didn't know how the Polish or German authorities would react to their illegal crossing.

One of the two women, Asta,[6] had known Veronica P. for a long time. Asta is an educated woman who has a gift for learning languages. After a few months in the Netherlands she was able to tell her story in Dutch. 'I lived in the same village as Veronica P., who seemed a normal housewife with children. I was invited to her house. After several visits, she suggested I could work in a German household. As life in Romania was bleak for me – I had problems with my job – the idea was appealing.' Asta finally decided to try it. Together with two other women from her village, who were also friends of Veronica P.'s, she went to Poland. Her party was divided between two cars, one driven by Veronica's husband. Until their swim there had been nothing illegal about the journey.

Before beginning their swim, they had been told to apply for political asylum in Germany, but they were refused political refugee status. 'No problem. There is another solution,' Veronica said.

They went to Turkish friends of Veronica's who had a bar. In Germany many night clubs and bars are owned by Turkish people.[7] Veronica arranged temporary employment for the women with them. In the bar the women's resistance was broken by food deprivation. If they wanted to eat they had to sleep with the clients.

A few days later the German police raided the bar and took Veronica, who was the only woman present at that time of the night. She was deported and the Romanian women were left on their own. However, this only lasted for a day because contacts of Veronica's had directed a fresh group of Turkish men to the bar. One of them owned a restaurant where the women were to work. Again they were taken by car. On their way Asta noticed that the signs by the roadside had changed. '"We must be in another country, probably in the Netherlands," I thought.' This trip ended at a pizza restaurant in a small Dutch village. She thought, 'At last, a normal restaurant.' But she was mistaken. 'The place had just changed ownership and nobody there had ever baked a pizza. Instead, it was a brothel in disguise which served Turkish customers only. The managers didn't advertise in the papers, but by word of mouth in Turkish coffee houses.

'We were made to understand that we had to entertain clients in a special way. To make it clear to the customers that they could sleep with us, one associate of the Turkish guys made a show of taking a woman upstairs. In the bedroom he did nothing, but just drank a glass of mineral water. He was not allowed to sleep with us; his job was to show clients that they could go upstairs with us.'

It was made clear to the women that if they didn't co-operate they would be taken somewhere worse and by worse the gang meant the whole litany of horrors involved in trafficking. The women were forced to give in.

The women were further threatened by the violence they had to witness. One day Asta came downstairs to see a man covered in blood. Knowing no better, she thought he was dead. She was forced to wipe up the blood. Only after she escaped did she learn that he had survived and had been abandoned, seriously wounded, in Germany. He was stabbed by a regular customer at the pizzeria, a Turkish man nicknamed the 'chicken doctor' because he could kill people as easily as he could slit a chicken's throat. (It emerged later that this fight had nothing to do with the women.) Veronica P. surfaced once more in the Netherlands to help out in the restaurant and it became clear that one of the Turkish men was her lover.

Asta kept resisting and was locked up as a result, while the other girls were allowed to go shopping. This was part of the divide and conquer policy of the traffickers. Not that they could buy much because they were never given any money, just cigarettes and food, as one of the suspects later admitted at the trial.

One day Asta saw a chance to escape and ran out to ring the neighbour's doorbell. From her window she had seen that a sympathetic-looking woman lived there. 'Please, polizei,' she said. The police raided the pizzeria on the same day. One of Asta's fellow victims was suspected of complicity because she hadn't been forced into prostitution, but Asta pointed out to the police that her situation was very difficult. A virgin when she arrived, she was then raped and reserved for the restaurant owner.

Obtaining the full story from the women proved difficult: some of the other girls had been promised Dutch husbands if they kept their mouths shut. No one could convince them that a paper marriage would not entitle them to stay in the Netherlands legally. However, when a suspect kept on threatening them, they finally realized that the trafficker wasn't trustworthy. The owner of the pizzeria had even taken the women to his lawyer to withdraw their statements formally: a highly irregular procedure, since a criminal defence lawyer is not supposed to meddle with his or her client's victims. At the trial the lawyer defended himself by saying that not he, but a trainee, had dealt with the Romanian.

At the end of the trial only the proprietor of the restaurant, Mustafa K., was sent to prison. At the trial he said he had been forced to exploit the pizzeria by a Turkish organization, which he did not dare to name. This could be true: some Turkish organizations like the PKK (the Kurdish Workers' Party) are known to extort money from Turkish citizens. Mustafa K. said he had been ordered to sell his poultry business to buy the pizzeria. Veronica P. was found guilty in her absence.

Turkish traffickers are involved in many of the cases involving Romanian women. Romania opened up not only to the west but to the east as well, to Turkey. On the other hand, the system works both ways. The Romanian mafia also plunder Turkish people as they wait in long queues on the Romanian-Turkish border. And Romanian and Turkish people work together in trafficking.

Are they taking over?

A madam of a brothel suspected that the Polish girl brought to her a few days earlier had not come of her own accord. The girl seemed terrified, so the madam called STV. I went to talk to her and, sitting on rubber sheets, the girl implored me to convince the madam that she was working of her own free will. She could not afford to lose her job because she had to earn £2,000 in the next two days – a sum no hooker could possibly hope to earn. If she couldn't pay up in time, her family would be killed. The madam refused to co-operate with the red mafia and took the girl somewhere else. She wanted to help, but wouldn't employ women under conditions like that. Nor did she like the idea of eastern European pimps waiting on her doorstep.[8] There have been other examples of sex-club owners asking for help the moment a girl is delivered. Another madam said, 'I don't want any trouble with the police. That's why I don't want Russian or Polish pimps to force girls to work in my joint, especially not when they are still under age. I send them away, but I know that other houses don't hesitate in hiring them.' A third brothel operator said, 'Every day I find a few eastern European women waiting on my doorstep.'

Health workers and other field workers have noticed a tense atmosphere in otherwise friendly clubs, 'especially when these eastern European creeps in tailormade suits enter the premises'. Prostitutes and their advocates report growing control by eastern European pimps in almost every red light district. A social worker in Rotterdam said, 'You can see them standing in front of the pros- titution houses. We don't know how long we can keep up our street-corner work.'

Since May 1994 the Dutch southern border region has had a special police force, which is solely concerned with the phenomenon of eastern European organized crime. Teamleader Jos Hermans and his assistants worked frantically in a room cluttered with computers: 'Indeed we have the impression eastern European criminals are taking over. Some big sex clubs have changed hands and are now owned by eastern Europeans. It all starts in a friendly way, with just two women being offered. Next these gangsters demand that the salaries of the women be paid to intermediaries, not directly to the women. Later on they brandish firearms and threaten to set the place alight. It doesn't just happen here. In a Frankfurt brothel six bodies were discovered, reputedly killed by the red mafia. In this part of the Netherlands we have to cope with Russian, Moroccan, German, Yugoslavian and even Dutch criminals. In this sparsely populated region there are twice as many sex clubs as in Amsterdam. We are making an inventory of 58 sex clubs. There are hardly any Dutch women working in these clubs. They work from escort agencies or their homes. The clubs each employ 30 women for a short space of time. Up to now we have found 325 illegal women, most of them from countries in central and eastern Europe. None of them work vol- untarily. We have only come across them by chance. Among them are only a few women from Ghana and Thailand. We encounter many "Polish" women who are in fact Russians. Then a few hours later a whole new team is turning tricks. These women cost very little: they are just throw-away merchandise. The gangs don't even take the trouble to select suitable women. Those who refuse are beaten up and disappear, we don't know where. We have never investigated escort agencies, but we have heard they employ young girls and boys from the Czech Republic.'

The core of eastern European gangs usually consists of four or five criminals of various eastern European countries working together. They are highly organized and have a strict division of labour: the recruiters don't take charge of the transportation to the brothels. On the whole eastern European women seem to be recruited by accident, by people they met by chance, for example in a café or on the street. The famous communist queues in front of shops have much to answer for: standing in lines offers great opportunities to contact people. The red mafia has also revitalized old tactics such as kidnapping and blackmailing women. Contrary to, for instance, Dominican cases of trafficking, family ties don't play a big part in the relation between recruiter and victim.

The Russian mafia is increasing its hold over surrounding countries. Trafficking in Russia has been taken over by redundant ex-army men, KGB officers and veterans of the Afghan War. Since the Berlin Wall came down it is estimated that more than 10,000 women have been working against their wishes in German prostitution. The red mafia is very active in Berlin. In Germany in 1993 200 organized eastern European gangs were at work.[9] Budapest is an important centre for the red mafia too. Small-scale traffickers take Romanian and Russian women there and then sell them to wholesalers.[10]

The break-up of the USSR increased traffic not just to western Europe but also to Turkey. Since the border with Georgia and Azerbaijan was opened up, people from the south of the former Soviet Union have invaded eastern Turkey, where women sell their goods as well as their flesh.[11] They have evoked the wrath of Turkish women, who accuse them of enticing their husbands. There was even a popular song about these 'Natashas'. Not enough women are volunteering for the job, so it is likely that many 'Natashas' are trafficked.[12]

The influence of the red mafia even extends to China, where it puts women to work in restaurants where they have to be nice to the customers and are paid for every kiss. Chinese men stand in line for their services.[13]

12 Mail-order marriage

'Europeans have the tempting idea that Asian women are very submissive. They think we are poor and therefore have to work in prostitution. I know many women have to, but not me,' said Gabriela, an Asian woman who was a mail-order bride.

Many women try to marry their way into industrialized countries, but they may find themselves living with a complete stranger who, more often than not, will be very hard to please. The trade in Third World brides, ordered through catalogues or introduction agencies, is increasing. Many agencies are genuine, but a small number don't care about their clients and are parties to the international trafficking of women. The women are trafficked in that they are completely dependent on the wishes of their husbands, who have bought them as if they were a commodity.

Most arranged marriages cannot be defined as trafficking. Often men want to meet women or women want to meet men and they do so using the services of an agency. In many cultures arranged marriages are the norm. In others matchmaking is a respectable institution, which works well provided the arrangement is undertaken on equal terms by both sides. However, there are agencies which don't care about the men and women they are introducing and which are only interested in making money. Some are known to take the money without arranging any introductions or to use photographs of women who don't want to marry.[1] Through others the woman is bought, without having the right to state her own wishes. Some European men who are genuinely seeking a wife complain of being showered with leaflets from unscrupulous agencies.

Such agencies can be recognized by the way they advertise the women – as submissive, or beautiful, or having no minds of their own. Where Third World women are advertised in the sex-tourist industry as promiscuous, in the mail-order bride business they are described as monogamous. The brochure for *Asian Contact*, which

has the revealing sub-heading 'Get a Posso in Your Life', says of
Asian women:

> Cheating on their husbands is an unknown phenomenon
> for them. Asian women can give you that little something
> that European women are lacking. They are affectionate and
> radiate an intense warmth and innocent coyness. They
> give you a lifelong friendship and real natural love. A man
> can feel himself a real man with them, something almost
> forgotten in Europe.

The brochure advertises women from the Philippines as Catholic
with western attitudes, well educated but traditional about matters
such as going out alone.

Future brides are recruited with promises of an easier life and
false arguments, for example that there is a shortage of women
in western industrialized countries prepared to marry men aged
over 50.[2] The brochures, in fact, are aimed at men in that age
bracket who feel they have missed out. One says, 'These women
consider it normal, even desirable that their husband is older than
they are. They think elderly men deserve respect.' Young men are
discouraged from applying, since they don't need agencies,
whereas young women are explicitly invited to join.[3] The women
can be ordered from a catalogue listing those who are available.
One suitor is known to have corresponded with no less than 700
potential future brides.

Some women will go so far as to marry a total stranger to
escape from a life without prospects; quite a few are obeying the
wishes of their family, who want them to better themselves. They
are placed in a very vulnerable situation, because in most European
countries they have to remain married for three or four years to
obtain a permanent residence permit. In Britain, for example, their
permit is set for only a year initially; many women remain illegally
for years in their husband's country because he does not register
them properly. Whether the legal length of stay permitted is one
or four years, the system gives the husband every opportunity to
pressurize or blackmail his immigrant wife with the threat of
divorce before the necessary period has elapsed. The way is opened
to abuse both in prostitution and in domestic labour.

One agency specializing in Latin American women claims its
merchandise is 'cheaper than a second-hand car and lasts longer'.
A leaflet advertising Brazilian women disparages Colombian
women: 'Brazilian women have a "western" countenance, whereas

Colombians don't. Brazilians are smaller and their faces are more refined. But they are expensive because they want to make phone calls to their families and to visit Brazil.'

Eastern European women are supposed to cost even less than South American women. They don't have to travel so far. Some clients prefer them because they are western looking. Polish women want western men 'because they drink less', and Russian women are said to be attracted by the same argument. The trade in Polish wives started in the mid 1980s. Mostly the husbands were farmers who couldn't find a Dutch, Belgian or British woman willing to share life on a farm. Polish women in the north of England have reported being subject to domestic violence.

Case histories

For under £100 the agency of the Filipina Conchita provided men all over the world with a catalogue of available women to choose from. The agency was based in the Netherlands but advertised for women in the Philippines. The men who replied weren't vetted and the women were given no choice about the men who were put in contact with them. Although the women didn't have to pay a fee, Conchita made a lot of money because she catered for hundreds of men. The women's wishes were irrelevant and there were no catalogues of marriageable men.

Priscilla, aged 35, was one of the women who responded to Conchita's advertisements in the Philippines. She had her own business and wasn't poor, but she had health problems and wanted medical advice and treatment. Priscilla sent her data to the agency. Her catalogue entry read: 'Miss Priscilla S. Weight ... , height ... , a Catholic with high school education, hairdresser by profession, would like to correspond with middle aged men.'

'That's how my marital problems with "John" started,' Priscilla told me, alternately indignant and laughing. 'He was the first to respond to my advertisement. He told me he had written to two other Philippine women. I was his third choice. After his appointment with me he was to meet the other women at the airport. I thought there was no harm in meeting him and we rented an apartment where we could spend some time together. Seven hours after he arrived he asked me to marry him. I said yes, providing he cancelled his appointments with the other two, which he did. We married in a hurry because he was about to lose his job, and if he was unemployed he said he could not get me a visa. I found out later that this was untrue. I wanted a marriage of convenience, which he agreed to. No sex.

'Later I found a postcard from one of the other two women. She had been waiting for him in a wedding dress and had arranged a big reception. She said on the card that she could kill him.'

When they arrived in the Netherlands John took Priscilla to a small, dismal, run-down house. She soon realized that John was using her to make money when a colleague of his told her, 'Your husband is a lucky man. Because he is married he gets social security for two, instead of for one. And he has a housekeeper for free as well.' Priscilla said, 'I was shocked. It was true. He wanted me to serve him all day long. I was not even allowed to watch television, the electricity was too expensive. He only gave me second-hand clothes and £3 a week to buy my own food, which was just enough to buy a little rice at the market. Sometimes I had to make some money for him on the side by doing other women's hair. He was too stingy to pay the bus fare, so I had to go on foot, sometimes a two-hour walk.'

John saved all his money for his holidays. Priscilla went with him twice. 'They weren't holidays, but trouble tours.' On these occasions she was treated badly. At night she was not allowed to sleep because she had to guard the car. John gave her 7 kilos of rice, which was just enough to last for two weeks. He let her look on while he ate alone in a restaurant.

On their second holiday they were accompanied by his 15-year-old daughter. Priscilla said, 'When I discovered he was abusing her sexually I decided to run away.' She realized that she was only a cover for his incestuous relationship with his daughter. With the help of a Dutch couple she ran away to the Netherlands. Later she filed for divorce. She brought a case against John, which lasted long enough for her to qualify for the crucial three-year residence period. The judge ordered her ex-husband to pay Priscilla the social security money retrospectively.

Priscilla's experiences are not unique. The marriages of two other migrant women were the cover for their husbands' serious problems. One discovered that her husband had tried to rape her daughter, who had joined them to keep her family together. He also had severe psychiatric problems. The other woman was blamed for her husband's gambling debts: she was falsely accused of having spent a fortune on the telephone, when in reality he had lost the money gambling.

The numbers of men with similar problems who hide them in marriage to a foreign woman are unknown. The majority of the husbands of mail-order brides have been married before. They frequently blame the breakdown of their previous marriage on the emancipation of their first wife, and hope wrongly that an Asian or other foreign bride will be more submissive. For instance, Gabriela from the Philippines said to me, 'My husband said western European women are lazy, expect you to work 16 hours a day and still complain about lack of money. At the time I agreed. But I know better now. Before I was a submissive Asian woman, but now I am an emancipated Dutch woman.' She added with amusement, 'Now he is divorced from a second emancipated woman, from ME.'

As a rule marriage agencies don't cater for bogus or paper marriages, which are only undertaken to obtain a residence permit for one of the partners, or in which one of the spouses may be acting honestly but may be exploited by the other. Some newly wed men have found their bank accounts plundered and their homes empty soon after the ceremony. Although bogus marriages don't fall under the heading of traffic in women, they are still used as a means for women to stay in the target countries.

Bogus marriages were common in the early 1980s. In 1983, for example, it was discovered that brothel-keepers were arranging marriages in Malaysia because in Thailand the authorities demanded too many papers to validate marriages with foreigners. In Malaysia they were less attentive.[4] In 1991 between 5,000 and 10,000 bogus marriages were still being arranged in a small country like the Netherlands. By 1993 the Dutch authorities had become more strict and only one was recorded.[5] Foreign partners now have to apply to the police and first have to be vetted by the Dutch embassy in their country of origin.

Some marriage agencies cater for the prostitution market directly, without bothering to find a bogus husband. In one case a mother and a daughter were recruited as secretaries for a marital agency, but at their destination they were forced into prostitution. Horrified, they left the country as soon as possible. A Russian woman who wanted to divorce her husband and return home was made to pay her fare back by working as a prostitute.

Nedya from Morocco is one example of the relation between arranged marriage and forced prostitution. When she married for the third time, she was made to prostitute herself under threat of being divorced before her three years' residence had elapsed. In Morocco she had been married and divorced twice, which meant that life there had become impossible for her. Her first husband divorced her solely because she gave him no sons. Nedya was left with three daughters to provide for. 'By the way, he married again and still has no son. Maybe his sperm is at fault,' she said cynically. She had never loved him. The marriage was arranged because her widowed mother could no longer afford to pay for her education.

'After that first divorce I didn't know how to make a living for myself and my daughters. For a while I took all sorts of odd jobs. I also became a domestic worker, but the woman of the house fired me because she thought I was making eyes at her husband, which wasn't true. Then I took on any job available in the neighbourhood.

'One day I met a fellow Moroccan who was on holiday, but lived in the Netherlands. I told him about my problems. We spent some time together. At one point he asked me whether I wanted to stay with him. I said yes, because I felt I had had enough of struggling on my own.' The man married Nedya, but didn't tell his parents. When they heard about it, they opposed the marriage because Nedya was a divorcee, which was synonymous with being a 'fallen woman'. What they didn't know was that their precious son had already been married to a Dutch woman and had divorced her. Neither did Nedya, by the way. His parents forced him to abandon Nedya, who didn't dare tell anyone that her marriage had failed again.

Fearing her family would find out, Nedya decided to go to Spain to sell trinkets to tourists. She arrived without a visa, but the Spanish immigration officers let her through because she had a little money on her. In Spain she encountered no problems but she didn't earn any money either. At last she met a trucker who offered to take her to Amsterdam. He was kind. He never harassed her or asked her for anything. He even bought her a rail ticket from Rotterdam to Amsterdam. There she found a job in a grill room. 'To reassure my mother, I phoned her to say I was all right. My ex-husband had also telephoned her to ask about my whereabouts, and my mother, who didn't know about the divorce, told him where to find me. I hadn't had the courage to tell her I was divorced again. So one day he walked into the grill room. He talked me into marrying him again and I agreed. He wanted me to quit the grill-room job.'

Nedya's happiness didn't last long. 'Soon I discovered that he needed a lot of money for his cocaine. He suggested that I work to pay for his drugs. According to him I could only stay in the Netherlands if I had a job, which was nonsense. I had a residence permit because of our marriage. I didn't mind working, but I didn't know how to set about getting a job. One day he showed me an advertisement for a sex club. I was angry. "If I had wanted to go on the game, I wouldn't have bothered to marry you," I told him. He said he would divorce me if I didn't do what he wanted, and divorce would mean I would be deported to Morocco immediately. I was scared, I could not go back after a third divorce. Still I didn't do what he asked. Then he started to beat me up.'

In desperation Nedya gave in. Her husband took her to a sex club, where she worked for a year. Whenever she said she wanted to stop he threatened to deport her. She had one more trick up her sleeve. If her daughter were to come to the Netherlands, she could argue that she had to stay at home to look after her. So one of Nedya's daughters joined them. That didn't work – Nedya was sent to the club anyway. Every night she took home a bag of French fries for her daughter, to prove that she worked in a snack bar, which is what she had told the girl. Instead of being easier, life became more difficult. Nedya couldn't risk leaving her daughter alone with her husband. Later she was unable to talk about the danger she thought her daughter was in. She could only say that she feared the real or attempted sexual abuse of her daughter.

Nedya worked less after the arrival of the daughter, which made her husband angry. To punish her, he threatened to send the girl back to Morocco to marry her off. Nedya could take no more. She decided to risk her residence permit. Her colleagues advised her to go to a Moroccan women's group. She made a statement to the police and was given a temporary residence permit. The case never came to court.

Nedya's life is much better now. She has a job and is learning Dutch fast. Her daughter is going to school. Her story is considered to be tinged with 'cultural idiosyncrasies', but she disagrees. 'Westerners are too quick to believe that our problems are inherent in our culture. What they mean is that they don't want to do anything about it,' she said angrily.

Moroccan traffickers

Arranged marriages play a major role in many cases involving Moroccan traffickers. Arranged marriage is not the same as forced marriage: when parents arrange a marriage they suggest a suitable candidate whom their son or daughter can refuse. It is assumed the two will get to know each other after the wedding. In a forced marriage either one or both of the marital partners have no say in the matter.

In some cases Moroccan traffickers who have Dutch residence permits introduce themselves to a girl's parents as a suitable candidate for marriage, or they pick up the pieces when an arranged marriage has failed. They concentrate on divorcees and other women who have to be married off, as happened in Nedya's case. The Moroccan recruiters have often lived in Europe for some time and don't have language problems. They are experts on both cultures and promise girls a good life in western Europe. Only two of the trafficked Moroccan women who were clients of STV had gone off alone and been picked up by European men who subsequently put them on the game. In four cases which came to STV's notice the women had been broken mentally by being hired out for sex to friends or relatives.

In other cases orphaned girls are taken in by a relative who is already working as a prostitute. So-called second-generation girls figure in yet another type of case. These are young women who have left their parents' traditional lifestyle in the Netherlands and drifted into the arms of pimps who manipulate them into prostitution.

Moroccan traffickers are sometimes involved in drug trafficking and quite often use their own merchandise. Most of them have records for other, non-organized crimes. There is only one case in STV's archives in which an internationally organized Moroccan gang expanded beyond small-scale traffic in women and drugs. A rich family enticed a girl to come to Europe. She had already given up her job in Morocco as a shop assistant because her father didn't approve of girls working outside the home. The rich family fenced cars and other goods and forged passports for new recruits, who in their turn were forced into prostitution.

In 1994 two young Moroccan women had the courage to sue members of another criminal Moroccan family for trafficking. Only one member of the family was subpoenaed. He was a corpulent boy of 22, dressed in an expensive leather jacket over a multi-coloured tracksuit. He was accused of trafficking the two women, car theft, house breaking, fraud with pay cheques and shooting one of his aides during a row: he shot the man twice, the second time presumably to remove the first bullet. He denied this last charge and claimed that his aide had been shot by someone else during a failed burglary.

His family were all in the public gallery in the court room, which was well guarded by armed policemen. There were also plainclothes policemen in the gallery, ready to stop any fighting between the clan and the girls' supporters.

The two terrified Moroccan women sat huddled together. 'They hardly dare to look,' a sister of the accused, who was sitting next to me in the gallery, whispered. Another relative said to the accused's mother, 'Stay calm, as soon as the trial is over these two sluts will go back to prostitution.' The mother, who was panting and unhealthy-looking, was dressed in traditional attire and was clearly the centre of the clan. Fortunately for the two women the judges emptied the court to hear their evidence behind closed doors.

Outside policemen tried to quieten the observers. 'Of course my mother is upset,' one daughter said angrily to a policeman. 'She is a widow and her innocent son is standing trial.' When the trial resumed, the public gallery was calmer. The boy on trial had been married four times and all the marriages reputedly had to do with trafficking. He married one of the victims twice, the other once. All the marriages were arranged with the girls' families. Before he married the two girls, he had already divorced a girl who might also have been forced into prostitution, according to the transcripts of police phone taps read out in court.

From these taps it also became clear that his mother had pressured the women and the others involved in the case to keep their mouths shut. Even the parents of one of the prosecution witnesses had been intimidated. On the morning she arrived in the Netherlands, the first victim was raped at the mother's house, locked up and at midday forced into sexual relations with friends. That same evening she was taken to a window brothel. Presently she divorced the boy, but he kept on pestering her. According to him, she asked him to marry another woman: 'She told me I was a good husband and that I should find myself a new wife, according to old Moroccan custom.' He decided to marry her friend. The marriage was arranged within a day.

A worse fate awaited the friend because he discarded her as soon as she arrived to live with him. She said in court, 'Only when I arrived in the Netherlands did I discover that his first wife was working as a prostitute. I married him because I assumed that in the Netherlands I could better provide for my family than in Morocco. At the border he handed me his first wife's passport, which was the only way for me to enter the Netherlands, he said. There we went straight to the house of his mother. There he deflowered me and showed me all sorts of paraphernalia for prostitution, like lingerie, condoms and vibrators. I first had to sleep with an older man who paid him. My husband had an air gun with which he first shot at the birds and next pointed at me.'6 She was also threatened by his family.

The boy ignored his second wife and eventually talked his first wife into remarrying him. He promised to stop using cocaine and better himself so that she could quit prostitution. She believed him, but after remarrying him she found that nothing changed and ran away with the help of a teacher who noticed she had been beaten up. The defendant claimed he had battered her because she was poisoning his food.

He was sentenced to three years in prison, but had the last word: 'I can only say, don't marry before you are 40.'

The British context

In other countries members of ethnic groups also abuse the system of arranged marriages to force women on to the game. This may be done openly or undercover, as seems to be the case in Britain. 'Ethnic communities are not exceptionally proud of it. In England forced prostitution of migrant women is cloaked with the respectability of family life. Some migrants are pimping. Sometimes a woman is made to sleep with brothers and friends for financial gain,' several women at the Asian Women's Resource Centre in London said. 'They are advertised by word of mouth. It is hidden behind family life, especially where extended families are concerned. The mother goes out to find her son a wife, who is sometimes treated as a slave. In-laws can cause women a lot of trouble. Most women from India and Bangladesh come for marriage. Women even pay to get married. Some of them buy a so-called agency visa, which doesn't entitle them to stay legally. There is much domestic violence. We know at least one woman who was forced into prostitution.'

Leslie Roberts of the International Anti-Slavery Society said, 'Eastern European women work on farms in the north as au pairs. It is never organized prostitution, but there is always a neighbour or a friend who sleeps with them. Many women are brought to the north for marriage. They are not part of the community, and when the marriage breaks up they have to work in prostitution.'

13 The trade in domestic workers

'When we enter the room, we wish you to leave and work elsewhere. Always present yourself in the black and white uniform. Open the door when Mr ———— or I arrive. Don't talk to guests. Just say hello and keep smiling.' These orders are taken from a set of handwritten 'rules of the house' for a domestic worker. The document, which was given to me by a worker at Kalayaan, a support group for enslaved domestic workers in London, does not date from the nineteenth century but was written recently by a *nouveau riche* using the sort of English that even a Dutch author can recognize as suspect.[1]

In Britain and on the continent it is the height of fashion to exploit a migrant servant. It happens, among other places, in Spain, Italy, France and Greece: the domestic helpers come from Bangladesh, Brazil, Colombia, Ethiopia, Eritrea, India, Indonesia, Morocco, Nepal, Nigeria, the Philippines, Sierra Leone and Sri Lanka. In Greece alone there are 40,000 domestic workers, 90 per cent of them women. Greece and the Middle East countries are notorious for their abuse of these workers.[2]

On the continent domestic workers are usually listed as 'au pairs', an institution originally set up to further cultural exchange. 'No way,' said 26-year-old Filipina Virginia, who was an au pair with a Dutch family. 'I had to iron till ten o' clock at night. When I finally met someone, I was not allowed to go out on my evening off.'[3]

Staff members of embassies don't have to use the au pair convention. Because they have diplomatic status they can easily circumvent the national rules for hiring domestic servants. The first cases of abuse of diplomatic staff in Europe were recorded in 1977. In the Netherlands at least one family with diplomatic immunity maltreated a domestic worker and locked her up. She repeatedly threw notes out of the window asking for help, but the police could do nothing because of the family's status. A member of another embassy escaped prosecution for exploitation and maltreatment by the skin of his teeth.[4]

Trafficking for purposes of domestic slavery and prostitution are related. When a woman is not successful as a prostitute, she may be turned over to a family as a domestic slave. STV has on file three reports of domestic workers who were trained to be prostitutes at the same time. In Belgium, for instance, au pair girls have been forced into prostitution.[5]

The United Kingdom

In a London flat, where I was staying and which was a refuge for victims of domestic slavery, a few Philippine women are telling typical 'domestic worker' jokes about Maria, who worked in Hong Kong. Because Maria's English was poor she made all kinds of comical mistakes. Through the jokes the Filipinas have found a way of coping with their difficult situation. They ran away from their employers because they could no longer stand the treatment they were receiving. They had entered the UK under the so-called Concession, an inbuilt exception to immigration law dating from 1991, which allows people coming to Britain to bring their own domestic staff. This was possible because the 1971 Immigration Act gave the Home Secretary wide discretionary powers. 'The Home Office was very clear about it. Britain needed business people from Hong Kong and Singapore, and they wouldn't come without their domestic workers. But even the immigration officers knew they were coming to work. Their stamp carried the formula "allowed to enter Britain",' said Brid Brennan, an expert who is working temporarily for the Transnational Institute in Amsterdam. She has been an active campaigner for domestic workers in the United Kingdom. 'Domestic workers came as tourists. A tourist visa forbids work, but the stamp also named the employer.' One of the women in the London flat had a stamp in her passport which stated that she was an unpaid worker.

This arrangement makes the women completely dependent on their employers. Annually 12,000 foreign women enter Britain under the Concession.[6] Exact figures as to how many are being exploited are not known, but it is at least 1,000 a year. Since 1991 there have been 4,500 documented cases of abuse in Britain.

As Brid Brennan said, 'The important difference between Britain and other countries is that the British government itself imports women. This is where criminalization extends to the government. Traffic in women is often done in corridors of criminality, but in Britain it is official. The United Kingdom criminalized women, but not the employers.'

A Philippine woman shows her wounded hands to another Filipina. 'My employer didn't allow me to use her washing machine. I had to do everything by hand, for hours on end. I'll never be able to work again,' she said at a meeting where abused workers try to help each other. Many of the women have similar stories to tell.

'I will cut your face and kill you if you disobey my orders. You are my slave,' one employer said to his domestic worker. If she tried to run away, he would have her killed. Another was not allowed to cry when she heard that her daughter had died. One employer had to go to hospital and made his servant sleep next to him on the floor. A nurse objected and offered her a bed, whereupon the girl's employer threatened to sack her if she accepted. Kneeling for two hours as punishment, eating off the floor, sleeping in garages, verbal abuse, being locked up: all these are standard items on the list of psychological and physical abuses domestic workers have had to suffer.[7] Some women have to sit on the floor when addressing their employers. Too many women reported that they could only sleep for a few hours each night, and that they could be woken up at any time. Wages are confiscated by employers. Letters are intercepted and women are denied contact with fellow countrywomen.

Confiscation of their passports ranks high on the women's list of abuse. Brid Brennan said, 'Many of the domestic workers do not have control of their own documents. When the employer approaches the immigration desk he gives up the woman's passport. That is the last time the woman sees it. She has no idea of her status. Some women were accused of stealing jewellery, but they weren't stealing, they were just looking for their passports. If a woman escaped, the employers would give her passport to her embassy. It emerged that the Philippine embassy had hundreds of passports, but they were not returned to the workers. The women wouldn't come to collect them for fear of deportation. Besides, they knew the service of the embassies to be bad.

'We call these women unauthorized. They came into the country legally, their stamp was clear. When they run away they become overstayers and can be deported. They survive by doing domestic work for well-meaning employers. We don't consider the women illegal. Illegals are individually responsible for their status. But the British government is responsible in this case,' Brid Brennan told me.

During the Gulf War a scandal emerged concerning the abuse of domestic workers by Kuwaitis who had fled to the United Kingdom. Brid Brennan again: 'At that time the problem intensified. Everybody thought the war was not going to be confined to Kuwait. They were badly protected. Most migrant workers had to stay behind and go without water, food or shelter for months. The workers wanted to leave. Why should they die in that stupid war? Kalayaan has many documented cases from that period, from all nationalities.'

'No one believes it,' said a Filipina who had experienced this at first hand. Despite her secretarial skills and a university education she could not make ends meet in her own country. So she decided to take a temporary job in the Middle East to make some money. Her eyes filled with tears when she remembered the humiliations she had suffered. She was beaten regularly, even by the children of the family. She could not understand why, but gathered it was because unknowingly she had broken the country's behavioural code. She was left to fend for herself when her Kuwaiti employer fled to England in the Gulf War.

In general, when employers move to the UK permanently or for a holiday, many women report an intensification of the problems. Once in Britain, the employers isolate the women further, probably to stop them running away. Still, quite a few have managed to get away, sometimes only in their nighties. Not all of them escape unharmed: one woman broke her pelvis and arm while climbing down a drainpipe. Another crawled through the cat flap.

Sexual abuse of domestic workers

Many of these women, 8.6 per cent of the 270 interviewed by Kalayaan, have suffered sexual abuse.[8] Sheila from Pakistan has managed to avoid 'things that men started to do to her', as she called it. These 'things' were to take place on her day off when associates of her employer took her to church and drove her home afterwards. 'Officially I was off on Sundays, but they just took me to mass. In the house where I worked there was another Pakistani lady. She overheard a man talking on the phone about plans "to do something to Sheila next Sunday". That Sunday after church they took me to work in a canteen. The employer had instructed them "to take Sheila and do with her what you want". They wanted to take me back to the house because they knew my employer would not be there. At first I thought they were joking. They thought I couldn't hear them, but I caught them talking about my price. I said, "Madam is not at home, so you are going to behave disrespectfully tonight." I said that I was there for the children, not to do something with men. They tried their best to come close to me. I thought, "I will be good to them, even if they are bad to me." I remained nice. That's why they didn't go through with their plans. They ended up feeling sorry for me.'

Sheila came to England in 1992. 'I have worked with rich families in Pakistan since I was ten years old. They treated me as their own daughter and encouraged me to learn things, but as yet I can't read or write. I knew a Pakistani family who wanted to bring me to England. At first I refused. Three years later they phoned me again from London and I accepted. To get a visa, I had to be interviewed at the English consulate. I expected to be happy in England. I thought my employer would be good to me because I was going to take care of her children. However, once I was in London they changed. My employer gave me a hard time. I was never happy. They didn't give me enough food. I could only eat the things that had gone off. Instead of throwing it away, they gave it to me. I could not go shopping by myself. I would have loved to sit in a park for a while. One time I was very sick. I felt dizzy and I had a bad cough. The family didn't send for a doctor but only gave me a tablet. The woman didn't let me rest. I was never finished. Once she treated me badly and set her husband against me. She pushed me against the door in a very painful way. I confronted them with their behaviour and packed my clothes. I didn't run away. I never run away from anything. But, they opened the door. I stood at the door. It was cold. I could go out, but they knew I wouldn't. Where to? I went in again. I was crying and asking God why. It is very painful to remember. After a year I was still there. That's why I feel fearful and ashamed. From then on they gave me an even harder time.

'I tried to find help. In church I met a Filipina woman, also a domestic worker. She had a good heart. I went to live with her. She was never rude to me and helped me with food and money.

My clothes are still with my employer. They'll have my things as a burden, when they leave for home.'

A small African woman was listening to this conversation. She also had quite a story to tell. As a child she was bought by a rich family. They took her to England and promised to educate her. They said she would have a better life if she would let her employer and his friends sleep with her. She didn't say whether she gave in or not. When she was growing into a woman she was even refused a bra. She threatened to commit suicide so they would have her body on their hands. That was effective and the family let her escape.[9]

All these abuses took place both in the Middle East[10] and in England. Businessmen from the Middle East who came to live in the UK brought their attitudes to domestic helpers with them. Brid Brennan said, 'This should not be seen in terms of Middle Eastern employers alone. Every nationality has used the loophole which the Concession offers. There have also been cases involving American, English, Chinese, Greek and African employers.'

'Why? Surely these employers are rich enough already. They don't need our meagre salaries.' This is the question that remains in the minds of many exploited workers. Sheila said, 'These employers wanted to frighten and weaken me. Strong people can punch you, weak people abuse you.' Kalayaan's Filipina educational worker Speedy said, 'In certain countries women are considered to be inferior to men. They take revenge on other women.'

In 1990 the case of an Indian woman, Laxmi Swami, against the Kuwaiti royal family was heard in an English court. Brid Brennan said, 'The Kuwaitis tried everything to have the case thrown out or to confuse the issue.' Laxmi Swami came to Britain under the Concession as the servant of the half-sisters of the emir of Kuwait. The princesses spent six months in Bayswater every year. When they were in a bad mood they kicked their servants. Laxmi and the other servants had to stand by the door when the princesses came home late at night. Laxmi's eyes were damaged because they had thrown keys in her face. She and another servant were beaten daily with a broom handle. The princesses also tried to strangle her with electric flex. Laxmi had to sleep in the corridor and to steal drinking water from the tap. She was permanently hungry. Plenty of food was thrown into the dustbin, but it was deliberately spoiled so she couldn't eat it. She managed to escape and took a taxi to the Indian high commission. From there she was sent back to Bayswater to get the taxi fare.[11] After five years she was finally awarded £300,000 in damages. Sri Lankan women had also run away from the same household. The princesses had several nationalities working together.

Mrs Swami's case was the start of a campaign initiated by women who had experienced similar treatment at first hand. The campaign has been carried by CFMW, the Commission for Filipino Migrant Workers, and Kalayaan. Kalayaan (Freedom) was founded because the campaign was extended to include domestic workers of nationalities other than Filipino. Kalayaan wants to restore the legal situation which existed before 1980, when migrant workers were not dependent on one particular employer and were eligible for a permanent residence permit after they had worked in Britain for several years.

Lord Hylton protested about the exploitation of domestic workers in Britain, which he described as slavery, in the House of Lords. The government introduced a few new measures, including a mandatory interview with a clearance officer at which the women are given an information leaflet. It seems unlikely that the women, who are completely dependent on their employers, would dare to talk about their problems. Many immigration officers are aware of the conditions the women have to work in. For example, one immigration officer asked an employer whether he took two Filipinas with him to have a spare if one ran away.[12] Further, girls are only allowed to enter the United Kingdom if their employers have paid them in previous months. Workers must be at least 17 years old. The Department of Employment has stated that abused domestic workers should have recourse to industrial tribunals and criminal litigation. But in reality they are unable to pursue claims or seek redress.

Saudi Arabia and the Lebanon

A small photo of a sombre-looking woman accompanies a newspaper clipping out of a Saudi Arabian newspaper, saying a Filipina is wanted by the police because she ran away from her employer.[13] In 1990 in Saudi Arabia 100 Filipinas were detained in deportation cells. King Fahd of Saudi Arabia is also alleged to be involved in a network which recruits slaves, according to his servants.[14]

In the Gulf region domestic workers comprise 20 per cent of the 6 million migrant workers who keep the economy going. After the oil crisis of 1973, the region became rich and a large labour force was needed to build a new infrastructure. People from Third World countries, where the cost of living had soared because of the rise in energy prices, needed the jobs.

Increased wealth created a desire for domestic workers as a status symbol, but, unlike other contract labourers, there were no regulations governing domestic workers – domestic work was not seen as productive.[15] At best these women were treated as members of the family, at worst they came lower in the hierarchy than the pets.

Filipina Flora, who is 31, has worked as a domestic worker in Saudi Arabia and the Lebanon, where she was stuck for six years because her employer would not let her go. Eventually the Red Cross paid a ransom to her employer. In her travels Flora experienced every problem a domestic worker can encounter. After having been sent by reasonable agencies to Japan and Saudi Arabia, she fell into the hands of a bad agency.

As a girl Flora had been kidnapped and forced to marry her abductor. The boy's father implored Flora's father not to make a statement 'because that would mean death row for him'. Flora gave in to retain her dignity, but the resulting marriage has never been happy. Her husband gambled and drank. Flora was resourceful; she sold biscuits in schools and made envelopes from waste paper. She then decided to end her unhappiness by taking a job abroad.

Flora first went to Japan with the rest of her family to work as an entertainer. The arrangements were made without a hitch; the money was a slight problem, but the family won this fight. Flora knew that many entertainers in Japan were forced into prostitution, but she wasn't. Then she heard there was work in Saudi Arabia. She applied and went as a domestic worker. There she met some problems, like the amorous advances of her employer, but she dealt with this easily because he was an elderly invalid.

She learned the strict rules which govern behaviour and dress. She had to wear the traditional costume and was not allowed to go out on the street alone. Even when living in other countries Saudi Arabian employers don't allow their domestic workers to speak with strangers outside the home. Flora stayed in Saudi Arabia for the full term of her contract. She was well paid and achieved her aim of providing for her family, which seemed all the more reason to look for a similar job on her return to the Philippines.

Through other people she heard of various opportunities. She didn't know where, but assumed they were in Dhahran in Saudi Arabia or Tehran in Iran. She applied and was hired because she had learned to speak Arabic. Flora signed a document stating she would pay the commission fee to the agency as soon as possible. After some weeks she learned that the agency had changed ownership and that the costs for brokerage had increased. 'Employees of the agency came to our home to see if we had sufficient valuables as collateral. They took the documents that proved we owned them. Unfortunately it was not enough. My mother had to sell a patch of land to pay the remaining fees. I still thought the agency was above board.'

Just before her departure, Flora learned that she was going to the Lebanon. As her family had gone to a lot of trouble, she didn't want to back out. After all, she wanted to get away from poverty and from her husband. When she arrived the Lebanese office of the agency tried to trick Flora by confiscating her contract and substituting a second one with harsher conditions. This is a common trick and many women sign the new contract in good faith, which is not in their own language but that of the country where they are to work. Fortunately Flora had a xerox of the original contract, but it was to prove no safeguard against future ordeals.

In the Lebanon the agency assigned Flora to two employers. The first was very nice and wanted to keep her and get rid of the agency, but because it would lose the fees both Flora and her employer had to pay the agency would not allow this. So Flora was assigned to a second household. She had to wait at the agency for her new boss to collect her. Only then did she realize how internationally orientated the agency was. There were women from Sri Lanka and Thailand waiting to be collected too. Flora said, 'We had to sleep in dormitories. The managers demanded sexual services from the women. I had a hard time keeping the boss at bay.' Flora befriended the Thai wife of one of the managers, who told Flora her husband tried to have sex with all women who arrived at the agency. She herself had been forced into prostitution by him.

From the other women Flora learned that working conditions were generally terrible in Lebanese households. The food was bad and they sometimes had to work 22 hours a day. Flora thought they were exaggerating. After all, her first employer from the same agency had treated her well. Why should the second one be worse? 'At last my second employer came to collect me. While he scrutinized me from top to toe, he said, "I dislike people who falsely accuse me."' The meaning of this ominous remark would become clear later. Flora was surprised and replied, 'Sir, I have only come to clean your house.' Bewildered, she went home with him.

'In that household I was only allowed four hours sleep a night. They didn't give me Sundays off, which I was entitled to. When I arrived they told me generously I could eat as much as I wanted. But that wasn't true. I wasn't allowed to take fruit or meat. I was only given leftovers. They had two children. Their father hit them and they in turn took it out on me. They kicked me when I was slow to obey them. Imagine, a ten-year-old child. They didn't even try to remember my name. When I wanted to discuss a domestic problem with their mother, they said plainly, "You can talk it over with us."

'My employer confiscated my passport and took my money, which he promised to send to my mother directly. She never got it. When I asked about it, he showed me the deposits in his own bank. I didn't buy that and said that I wanted proof he had sent the money to the Philippines. I knew nobody in the Lebanon. I didn't even know the name of the town where I was working. I only had the telephone number of the agency. But when I phoned the mistress of the house listened in on her extension.

'When the family went out, the other servants and I were locked up. The employer showed us a gun he said he would use if we tried to run away. When we really had to go out, the employer sent bodyguards along with us.'

For Flora, her worst experience was her employer's attempt to rape her. One day he asked Flora if she would clean his office before the other employees arrived. He made a pass at her, but she pressed herself against the window. She claimed she would break it and pull him through with her if he went any further. Flora said, 'I played for time. I was bluffing, but eventually he let go of me.' However, this incident didn't prevent him from a second attempt at sexual intimidation. One night the small son came to Flora's room and told her his father needed her. The boy implored her to obey because he would be beaten up if she refused. It wasn't a glass of milk the father wanted, but sex. Again Flora managed to escape by the skin of her teeth. She complained to his wife, who didn't believe her. This backfired on her. 'I am falsely accused, and you know I don't like that,' the husband said.

By now Flora's position had become impossible. She planned to escape with another servant who was in the same predicament. They decided to run away while walking the dogs. They put their belongings in plastic bags so that they could pretend they were putting the rubbish out. The plan nearly failed. A neighbour saw them, but she couldn't tell Flora's boss in time.

The two Philippine women hailed a taxi and asked the driver where they could go. He took them to a place where many foreigners gathered and where they met an African teacher who took care of them. This couldn't last long. The other servant went her own way, and Flora had to fend for herself. She couldn't leave the country because her former employer still had her passport. She asked for it several times, but he would only give it to her after she had paid the expenses he said he had incurred because she had run away.

Flora had a hard time. She kept house for people who could only give her food and shelter. Shelter it was, because at the time the Lebanon was being bombed heavily and Flora literally had to pick up the pieces. She managed to contact her sister who lived in Europe, who warned the Red Cross. Eventually they paid the money to release Flora. 'Some story,' Flora concluded. 'I want to tell it again and again, because I am not the only one.'

Now she lives in a village with her second husband, who is Dutch. She still suffers from stomach disorders as a result of the abuse she suffered but that doesn't prevent her from cooking a good meal for anyone who visits her, including me.

Economic dependence of sending countries

Illegal agencies such as the one Flora went to are a legacy of the Marcos regime. President Marcos saw contract labour as an important source of foreign revenue, and in the early 1970s founded the Overseas Employment Development Board to keep the recruitment of such labourers in his control. Since 1983 Filipinos working abroad have had to remit a large part of their earnings to special government banks, which charge them high commission. Private agencies avoided these remittances.

The Board should have made these private agencies redundant. However, it could not cope with the volume of job applications and so in 1982 Marcos created the POEA, the Philippine Overseas Employment Agency, which also in its turn became overburdened. After that private citizens and illegal agencies filled the gap. When President Aquino came to power she did nothing to curb the activities of these agencies but, on the contrary, expanded the policy of labour export.[16]

Illegal agencies hire people directly without completing the necessary documentation. The agencies often lend the women the money for their own recruitment fees and take their passports as collateral. The women are supposed to pay up just to have their documents back for a short span of time. They need them to show at the police station, for example, or at the bank. Agencies often recruit in five-star hotels. Sometimes families have to pay money to agencies which only pretend to find them work. Usually the unlicensed agencies promise a backdoor departure to avoid the government authorities, for example by boat and not via Manila airport.[17]

The two women I met in London, who were making jokes about Maria in Hong Kong, talked about their experiences with these agencies. 'They don't care if you speak English. You just have to answer some questions which are videotaped. One of us even had to pretend she had a high-school education. She didn't even know how to spell "high school".' The women go abroad completely unprepared: 'I also had to undergo a medical check-up. I had X-rays for the first time. I had to undress several times. I didn't know why.' Women going to Hong Kong are made to have a pregnancy test.

The Philippines receive yearly £1.3 billion remittance money from overseas workers, which may help some families but in general doesn't benefit the poor. Some critics claim that remittances have produced negative effects like inflation, and rises in the price of rural land, the cost of labour and imported goods. They also create a political dependence on the receiving country. The governments of the sending countries hardly ever oppose human rights abuse in the receiving country. Only recently, due to domestic pressure, the Philippines had to take action against Singapore when the domestic worker Flor Contemplacion was convicted of murdering her employer and hastily executed with little investigation. Other Third World countries also encourage their women work abroad to remedy their budget deficits. Singapore profits directly from domestic workers. Employers have to pay a 'levy' to the state, which gives them an excuse to pay the women less.

Remittance money also boosts the economy of Sri Lanka, where wages plummeted after the economy was liberalized. Sri Lankan women went as domestic workers to countries which women from other nationalities were avoiding because of bad publicity about exploitation.

Domestic work and prostitution apart, Third World women have also been sold as surrogate mothers. Even dead women have become merchandise. Until a few years ago in Japan, it was possible to insure the life of a third person. If he or she died, the person who bought the insurance would benefit. Some 50 unsuspecting Filipinas' lives were insured in this way; 18 of them died in freak accidents. They are believed to have been murdered by Japanese organized crime, the yakuza.[18]

Another form of trade – in human spare parts – came to light in India in 1988. A woman from Bangladesh escaped from a hospital just before her kidneys, liver and other useful organs were about to be removed. She and fellow victims, who had died, had been bought for no more than £60. They had been deceived with false promises of domestic labour. Nearer home there have been some alarming reports about traffickers in kidneys.[19] Elsewhere the Russian mafia are setting up in the trade in human organs.[20]

14 Nobody's business

'It is time you did something about traffic' – one of my interviews ended abruptly with these words. The woman's anger was justified. Despite various proposals to stop traffic in women, it is still widespread. The measures put forward always reflect the differing views of the problem: as a violation of human rights, as a migration-related problem, as part of serious organized crime, or as a result of prostitution policy. It is also seen as a consequence of war.

'Guess what was indicated as one of the main causes of traffic in women? Militarism. No further explanation needed,' a journalist at the foundation of an international network against trafficking in 1983 complained. However, there is no reason to disparage the connection between militarism and traffic in women. The Vietnam War was one example, the supply of women to the American bases in the Philippines another. Reports from the war zones in former Yugoslavia suggest that traffickers are active there.

When traffic in women is seen as an infringement of human rights, two types of measure are usually called for: reformulation of international conventions and better economic conditions for women. Some international treaties apply to traffic in women but don't mention it explicitly, for example the Universal Declaration of Human Rights and various anti-slavery treaties. The most recent international treaty concerning traffic in women dates from 1949 and has been ratified by 60 countries. It consolidates all previous treaties:

> The Parties to the present Convention agree to punish any person who, to gratify the passions of another:
> 1   Procures, entices or leads away, for purposes of prostitution, another person, even with the consent of that person.
> 2   Exploits the prostitution of another person, even with the consent of that person.[1]

The treaty therefore condemns *any* mediation in prostitution by a third party. The Netherlands, for instance, refused to ratify it because of this unrealistic approach to third parties who organize a place for prostitutes to meet their clients. Such third parties have to be accepted if a society tolerates prostitution. The treaty also rejects women who enter prostitution voluntarily, echoing the absolutist stance of those abolitionists who believe that all prostitution is reprehensible and women should not need sex work as a vocational option. As a result, in some countries women's groups are reformulating this treaty, to recognize prostitution and informal jobs such as domestic work as labour.

Better economic status for women might prevent traffic altogether. In 1980 the United Nations estimated that women do two-thirds of all the work that has to be done on this planet, but receive a tenth of the proceeds. They own only 1 per cent of the world's capital. 'Traffic in women should be remedied in the Third World, not here,' is one common opinion on the subject. However, although poverty plays an important part in trafficking, it isn't the only reason for it.

As a rule traffickers in people don't concentrate on the poorest countries but on women from newly industrialized countries like Thailand and the Philippines. Thai women became unemployed after they had to give up small-scale land cultivation to process export-quality rice industrially. Traffic-prone women are the women who are almost the poorest who spend their meagre savings on middlemen or accept their parents' offer to sell their last patch of land.

Responsibility towards the extended family may be an important factor in a country that expects much from migration. For some Philippine women the scales in favour of migration were tipped by the needs of their families.[2] 'For a family in the Philippines it is important to have at least one son or daughter working abroad,' explained the Philippine psychologist Rohlee de Guzman, who has first-hand experience of this phenomenon. 'A son or a daughter working overseas offers a chance to survive in the Philippines' dwindling economy. Mostly the eldest children feel the burden of this responsibility. That's why Filipina nurses leave the country for jobs below their intellectual ability. My neighbour in the Philippines had got herself a job as a domestic worker in Hong Kong. She took her 15-year-old daughter with her. This mother reproaches her other daughter for having married a Filipino instead of accepting a job abroad.'

Migration of women has a great social impact. 'From the Philippines there are many reports of incest, especially in families with a mother working abroad,' according to Rohlee de Guzman. 'More and more parents realize their daughters work in prostitution, but they consider it as part of the deal, as long as the women come home safely.'

Many migrant women in Europe have to pay for their parents' old age with money earned from prostitution. Colombian Marcia is one of them. 'Still, it is better to be exploited by your family than by traffickers. Your family is grateful and you can see how they spend it.' Most women who come into contact with social workers state lack of opportunity as their motive for migration and, sometimes, for their decision to enter prostitution. 'We are poor and I wanted to help my family' is the standard opening in interviews with most migrant prostitutes. Women from the Third World are supposed to become prostitutes solely because of grinding poverty, but there is more to it than that. When traffickers can, they work on women who are in a difficult situation.

Quite a few of the women I interviewed have problematic backgrounds of forced marriage and sexual or physical abuse. For instance, Colombian Marcia, who was trafficked by Manuel, was sexually harassed by her stepfather when she was 13 years old. She also had to work in the house from three o'clock in the morning till late at night. She married as soon as possible just to escape from her home. Her husband battered her and she ran away to become a prostitute. She remarried, this time to a drug trafficker. This marriage didn't work either, and at the time of the separation she knew too much about the drug trade and had to make a run for it. Then she met Manuel, who opened up new horizons for her. Her friend Ana, from the Dominican Republic, was raped by her boyfriend as a young girl. Her father forced her to marry him, which was the start of a sequence of abuse. She left home to work in restaurants, where she entertained clients. She decided marriage to a foreigner was the only way out.

As a child, Tina, who lived in the poor northern border region of Thailand, had to leave her home because her father was caught trafficking drugs to Burma. Her fosterparents maltreated her and the sons attempted 'to kiss her' when she was in bed. When she took a job in a factory, she was exploited badly. Later she decided to let men pay for the things they did to her. At this point a contact she made with a Dutch sex-club owner was more than welcome. She went to Prague and ended up imprisoned in a Dutch brothel.

In any population of prostitutes there is a percentage with similar backgrounds.[3]

Europeans and Americans are biased in their attitudes towards Third World prostitutes. Furthermore, to the dismay of western prostitutes, social scientists tend to neglect their economic motives, but emphasize their maltreatment and childhood abuse in making their decision to enter prostitution.[4]

Forewarned is forearmed

'Imagine you live in a Philippine village. A helicopter lands with the name of well-known cigarette brand on it. A few men in expensive suits descend. They address village girls and offer them jobs as domestic workers. What are these girls supposed to do? You can warn them, but the prospect of a better life deafens them to well-meaning advice. They'll most likely think that you are talking them into missing the chance of their lives,' a social worker, who has lived in the Philippines for years, said.

She is right. The effects of public education are limited. Women tend to think it will happen to someone else, not to them. For example, Fatima from Indonesia who was trafficked by the Billionaire gang was explicitly warned by her brother against traffickers, and so was able to recognize trafficking when she experienced it. Hopefully women who have been alerted to its dangers will recognize traffic in time to escape it.

In 1993 Dutch experts made an educational soap opera to deter Dominican women from coming to Europe. The film features a woman who is not trafficked, but finds herself in big trouble in prostitution. 'Whenever that movie is shown, we see an increase in women from the Dominican Republic coming to the Netherlands,' a police spokesperson commented. 'It just advertises the possibility of getting rich in European prostitution.' However, the soap had an interesting side effect. Parents became worried about the fate of their daughters who had migrated abroad and founded a parents' group to discuss the effects of prostitution.

Dutch experts have plans to target eastern European countries with a similar film, but it won't be easy. Prevention in eastern Europe has to overcome specific hurdles. Eastern European women are not affected by the argument that they will be illegal aliens in the west. Under communism everyone was involved in something illegal and many people are proud of their underground activities, which often contributed to the downfall of communism. Labour relations in eastern Europe still bear the scars of this attitude towards the authorities. Future victims of traffic don't question their prospective foreign employers because they come from a culture where it was useless to criticize the bosses. The Russian motto 'We pretend to work and they pretend to pay us' sums up this state of affairs.[5]

Visa regulations

Restrictions on movements of people, which would limit transfers inside the European Union, are often called for to repress traffic in women. However, limiting mobility goes against the European policy of opening inner borders and is also not feasible in many countries. Leen Pieterse of the Dutch Criminal Intelligence Unit commented, 'Every hour some 1,000 vehicles cross our borders. You'd have to install an army of policemen at the frontiers just to stop the 10 per cent of tourists who have criminal intentions. You'd create the same ominous and eerie atmosphere you used to feel visiting a country behind the Iron Curtain. Then each tourist had to state exactly where he was going to spend each night.'

The other possibility, stricter visa regulations, would merely drive the traffickers to use other routes. If for example the Dutch authorities state that Colombians need a visa to enter the Netherlands, then the traffickers will target countries like Denmark which don't have visa requirements. Traffickers try to avoid visa regulations by making complicated detours. In 1993 a group of Philippine women travelled via Bangkok, nominally to Istanbul and Morocco. They had to change planes at Schiphol airport and their flights had been arranged so that they had to wait overnight at Schiphol for their connection. The traffickers knew that, for humanitarian reasons, the authorities allow passengers to leave the transit room when they have to wait a whole night. When the women were let out the traffickers had a bus waiting to take them to the red light district in Antwerp.[6] According to the Dutch immigration police at Schiphol, many Philippine women travel via Morocco or other countries where Filipinas don't need visas. Stricter visa regulations merely create new challenges for organized crime.

What do the victims stand to gain from police interference, the investigation and the resulting court case? A trial is an ordeal from which the women themselves hardly ever benefit; they can only recover a small fraction of the money they are owed. Still, a trial is public recognition that they have been wronged. Unfortunately in many countries women aren't given the chance to wait for the case to come to court.

It is possible to bring a civil lawsuit for breach of contract. Women are not allowed to remain in the country until the case is heard, although they can stay for a criminal case. Domestic work is also unregulated. The London solicitor Jean Gould, who has undertaken many cases for domestic workers, said, 'Working in a private household is not considered labour. The women can only charge their employers with physical abuse, not for their unpaid labour. They are not entitled to an income. We sue employers by a different means, for breach of contract. Employers ignore written contracts, which the agencies and the employers have fixed together. False imprisonment comes under the heading of assault. Another offence is intimidation, which has long been unused but has recently been reactivated. Intimidation can be a threat: it boils down to using unlawful force and coercion.

'In one case I got £50,000 for my client, but most cases are settled out of court. You have to find a balance of proof. I sue employers for physical or psychological damage. But the worst cases of abuse are difficult to prove.

'Victims don't have the right to stay in the UK to await their trial. There is no clear policy. But there is discretion around the rule that people can sue for damages in civil cases. The victims are only allowed visitor's status, so they can't apply for social security to maintain themselves. The Criminal Injuries Compensation Board only awards compensation for the results of crimes of violence.' Several campaigns have now been set up to recognize domestic work as labour and to ensure these workers are paid a basic minimum wage.

Fighting the traffic in women through criminal and civil law is costly and time-consuming. Sex workers have problems in bringing civil lawsuits because prostitution is not recognized as labour. The woman has to prove that she was hired for another job with a salary. This same problem affects trafficked women.

In most countries the laws concerning traffic in women are part and parcel of the legislation on prostitution. Legislators have often held the abolitionist or regulatory view. However, repression of prostitution has been proved not to work and to be very costly. In the United States in 1985 the 16 largest cities spent on average $7.5 million on enforcing prostitution laws. Many municipal governments spent more money on controlling prostitution than on education or public welfare.[7] The abolitionist position which leads governments to prohibit prostitution altogether, or the weaker version in which the state refuses to tolerate prostitution, are still prevalent in western Europe and the United States.

Their failure to be pragmatic is not the only reason why abolitionists are increasingly isolated. Abolitionists refuse to listen to their opponents. At the founding of the international network against traffic in women in 1983, advocates of prostitutes' rights were forbidden to speak, and this position has not changed over the years. However, it is being challenged increasingly, for example by the International Anti-Slavery Society. Leslie Roberts, spokeswoman for the London branch, said, 'Abolitionism marginalizes the women. In no other group are the victims asked to shut up, not even when it concerns abused children. We want to widen the debate. It is important to hear the other side, the point of view of the women themselves.'

Countries like Germany, India and the Netherlands tolerate prostitution and want to regulate it in the public interest. This may be achieved by the institution of state brothels, as in Turkey or in Germany's eros centres. Women can be sold to these institutions or may have to buy themselves in. Countries which adhere to the regulatory view as a rule formally forbid living off the proceeds of prostitution but don't condemn private transactions between prostitutes and their clients. Since, in practice, this can prove to be contradictory, demands have been made that the sex industry in, for instance, Germany, the Czech Republic and the Netherlands be legalized. This is the third option, after toleration and prohibition. The Dutch police officer Jos Hermans said, 'Before you start criminal investigations, you'd better meet the first requirements. First legalize prostitution, then start fighting traffic in women. Treat prostitution as labour and give the women contracts. When criminals bring their girls, you can ask for their papers. You just send them away if they don't have them. Then we can concentrate on the excesses that will still occur in underground circuits.'

Hans Scholtes of the Institute for Prostitution Affairs said, 'You have to make the sex industry visible as you can't stop migration. I have proposed starting a legal, non-profit-making employment agency for all prostitutes. This agency will know where and in what circumstances they are working. Such an agency would short cut the activities of criminal gangs.' Scholtes' idea fits in with the thinking of the VER, the Dutch association of owners of relax-houses. 'Such an agency should be explicit about the kind of job being offered and take care of decent housing,' Klein Beekman, the chairman, said. Priscilla Alexander of the National Task Force on Prostitution in the United States agrees with this view: 'I think you should regulate debt bondage without extortionate interest. So these women have a kind of credit card for the real cost. It should be a kind of indenture, a mutual convenant.'

The problem is that legalization only institutionalizes the owners of brothels. Legalization alone is inadequate because working conditions also have to be changed. When no one but the prostitute herself can rightfully pocket her earnings, there will be no reason to traffic women for prostitution. This is the only way to curb the power of criminal sex-club owners and it is also where the fight for better working conditions currently being waged by prostitutes' rights movements comes in. They want to own their own businesses and control their working conditions without having to pay a large part of the takings to brothel-owners. Sex workers want to determine their working conditions, where and when they work and which customers they accept or refuse. In other words, they want to retain their sexual autonomy. They also consider prostitution to be a profession in which women should be allowed to work anywhere in the world for reasonable pay.

Since traffickers continually find ways around the limitations imposed on migration to Fortress Europe, the abolition of all immigration laws might seem to be the answer for migrant prostitutes. It is certainly the answer proposed by the English Collective of Prostitutes. Niki Adams and Nina Lopez of the ECP said, 'Migrant women come to Europe to relieve their poverty. Give them the right to enter and to work and traffic will vanish.' Priscilla Alexander expresses similar views: 'Traffic will continue until we get legalized.' From the beginning of the 1980s onwards Priscilla has stressed legalization of prostitution as the key to eradicating exploitation in the sex business. 'When the women can get a legal job, they don't have to pay these intermediaries. For us it is a migration issue, it has to do with restrictions on migration. That is why these women have to work in the illegal sweatshops in the garment industry. These places have at least 100 women working behind locked doors. The same holds good for the toy industry. I know some women, even young girls, think that is worse than being a sex worker. It is all one and the same market.'

They may be right, but the European Union will never open up its external borders to offer employment to everyone. Besides, it won't be the solution to trafficking. Women who enter a country as brides or domestic workers are trafficked on the margins of the sex industry. Many women arrive who don't want to work as a hooker and who may not even want to live abroad. They are ashamed of the job and consequently easy to blackmail into handing over their earnings. They should be given support and the right to sue their tormentors. Women who have been trafficked need support, otherwise they won't come forward and traffic will remain invisible. Non-govermental organizations have a role to play here.

The women need a refuge while they consider whether to press charges against the traffickers. They have to come to terms with their memories of their experiences and phrase them carefully to the police. Next they have to gauge the risk of reprisals against their families. They should be given a voice without placing themselves in jeopardy. First and foremost, the existence of traffic should be recognized. When its victims speak up, they should not be met with a deafening silence.[8]

Any woman, whether or not she is a prostitute, whether she is unemployed in Europe, toiling to keep a family in Africa, or an eager student in Latin America, who wants to escape a life without a future, to escape from drudgery or tradition, can become a victim of trafficking. Global trafficking is a hidden scandal which abuses women in their struggle to emancipate themselves and their families.

Addresses

AGISRA,
Niederichstrasse 6,
50668 Cologne,
Germany

AGISRA,
Wankstrasse 7,
812 Weilheim,
Germany

AGISRA,
Kasseler Strasse 1A,
60486 Frankfurt-am-Main 90,
Germany

Anti-Slavery International,
Unit 4,
Stableyard,
Broomgrove Road,
London SW9 9TL
UK

Batis Center for Women,
Room 711, Don Santiago
  Building,
1344 Taft Avenue,
Ermita,
Manila,
The Philippines

EMPOWER, Chiang Mai,
136/3 Ratchamaka,
Muang,
5000 Chiang Mai,
Thailand

Foundation for Women/WIC,
P.O. Box 47,
10700 Bangkoknoi,
Thailand

Frauen Informations Zentrum
  (FIZ),
Landhausstrasse 62,
70190 Stuttgart 1,
Germany

Frauen Informations Zentrum
  (FIZ),
Quellenstrasse 25,
8005 Zurich,
Switzerland

GABRIELA-National,
P.O. Box 4386,
Manila 2800,
The Philippines

Kalayaan,
St Francis Community,
Pottery Lane,
London W11 4NQ
UK

Le Nid,
14 rue Hydraulique,
1040 Brussels,
Belgium

Payoke-Saralek,
Zirkstraat 27,
2000 Antwerp,
Belgium

Polish Feminist Association
  (PSF),
ul. Mokotowska 55,
skr Pocztowa 30 00–504,
Warsaw 15,
Poland

Saalaa: House for Women,
143 Shimohirama Saiwai-ku,
Kawasaki-shi,
Kanaga-ken 211,
Japan

Stichting Tegen Vrouwenhandel (STV),
P.O. Box 1455,
3500 BC Utrecht,
The Netherlands

Notes

1 The characteristics of traffic

1 Bel Acceuil, a group of abolitionists, talks about millions of victims. The All Nepal Women's Organization estimates that on a world scale 30 million women are sold. 'Worldwide 200 million people are living in conditions of slavery. The United States also has its sex slaves,' American news network CNN, 9 March 1993. 100 million slaves worldwide is another number quoted. *Dagblad von Noord-Limburg*, 28 April 1992.
2 See the publication by Licia Brussa.
3 Wagenaar, Agnes and Velde, Feikje van der, 'Vrouwenhandel, een moderne vorm van slavernij', paper, Amsterdam, March 1990.
4 Bovenkerk, Frank, *Hedendaags kwaad: criminologische opstellen*, Amsterdam, 1992.
5 In STV's archives.
6 *Fortean Times, The Journal of Strange Phenomena*, no. 7.

2 Traffic old and new

1 Mancini, J.L., *Prostitutes and Their Parasites: An Historical Survey*, London, 1963.
2 Balkestein, J., *Dossier over de handel in vrouwen en meisjes*, 1901–2, in the archives of Meester A. de Graafstichting, Institute for Prostitution Affairs, Amsterdam.
3 Roe, Clifford, *The Great War on White Slavery*, 1911, and Miner, Maude E., *Slavery of Prostitution: A Plea for Emancipation*, New York, 1916.
4 O'Callaghan, Sean, *Der weisse Sklavenhandel*, Berlin and Vienna, 1967.
5 Bristow, Edward J., *Prostitution and Prejudice: The Jewish Fight against White Slavery, 1870–1939*, New York, 1982.
6 Lecture by Anna Stadaucher, conference in Prague, November 1993.
7 Barlay, S., *Die Sexhändler*, Vienna and Hamburg, 1967.

8   Roe, *The Great War on White Slavery*.
9   Cited in Barry, Kathleen, *Female Sexual Slavery*, New York, 1981.
10   Ibid.
11   Bristow, *Prostitution and Prejudice*.
12   Barry, *Female Sexual Slavery*.
13   Walkowitz, Judith R., *City of Dreadful Delight*, Chicago, 1992.
14   Collard, W.L.A., *De handel in blanke slavinnen*, Amsterdam, 1900.
15   O'Callaghan, *Der weisse Sklavenhandel*.
16   'Vice' in BBC documentary series, *The Underworld*.
17   O'Callaghan, *Der weisse Sklavenhandel*, and Barlay, *Die Sexhändler*.
18   This period is best documented by Barry, *Female Sexual Slavery*. See also *Nieuw Linie*, Amsterdam, 23 April 1975. Eros centres are huge brothels that may contain 200 or more prostitutes.
19   *Quod Novum*, Rotterdam University, April 1982.
20   ISIS, *Let Our Silenced Voices Be Heard, International Information Pack*, series no. 3, March 1993.
21   Various books on the subject: Branssen, Els, *Vogelvrij: prostituti-etoerisme en vrouwenhandel*, Utrecht, 1984; Latza, Berit, *Sextourismus in Suedostasien*, Frankfurt-am-Main, 1987; Lipka, Susanne, *Das kaufliche Glück in Sudostasien: Heirathandel und Sextourismus*, Munster, 1985; Roerink, Alide and Vleuten, Nelleke van der, *Handel in illusies: prostitutietoerisme in Thailand*, Nijmegen, 1988.
22   Asian and Pacific Development Centre, *Trade in Domestic Helpers: Causes, Mechanisms and Consequences, Selected Papers from the Planning Meeting on International Migration and Women, Quezon City, Philippines, 30 November–5 December 1987*, Kuala Lumpur, 1989.
23   Branssen, *Vogelvrij*.
24   *Travel Market*, 3 May 1982.
25   In STV's archives.
26   ISIS; Enloe, Cynthia, *Bananas, Beaches and Bases: Making Feminist Sense of International Politics*, London, 1989.
27   ISIS.
28   Vulto, Marij, *Een Kwestie van Overleven*, report by Meester van Graafstichting, Amsterdam, 1983.
29   *Nieuwsbrief STV*, no. 2, November 1990.
30   BBC, *Panorama*, 2 December 1983.
31   *Volkskrant*, Amsterdam, 3 December 1988.

3   A global brothel in a global village

1   *Folha de Sao Paulo*, Brazilian newspaper, 17 July 1993.
2   According to a representative of a human rights organization, *Dagblad van Noord-Limburg*, 17 June 1993.

3   ISIS, *Let Our Silenced Voices Be Heard, International Information Pack*, series no. 3, March 1993.
4   Ibid.
5   Ibid.
6   Gronewald, Sue, *Beautiful Merchandise: Prostitution in China, 1860–1936*, New York, 1982.
7   ANP, Dutch press agency, 15 August 1992.
8   *Volksrant*, Amsterdam, 16 February 1993.
9   *Arnhemsche Courant*, 8 July 1991.
10 Kaplan, David E. and Dubro, Alec, *Yakuza*, Utrecht, 1987.
11 Ibid.
12 *Brabants Dagblad*, 16 February 1994.
13 Bovenkerk, Frank, *Hedendaags kwaad: criminologische opstellen*, Amsterdam, 1992.
14 Asian and Pacific Development Centre, *Trade in Domestic Helpers: Causes, Mechanisms and Consequences, Selected Papers from the Planning Meeting on International Migration and Women, Quezon City, Philippines, 30 November–5 December 1987*, Kuala Lumpur, 1989.
15 Kaplan and Dubro, *Yakuza*.
16 Shizuko, Ohshima and Francis, Carolyn, *Japan through the Eyes of Women Migrant Workers*, edition of HELP, Asian Women's Shelter, Tokyo, 1989.
17 TVI documentary, France, 2 March 1994.
18 *De Stem*, Dutch regional newspaper, 5 July 1993.
19 In the 1900–18 period many Chinese girls, sold by their parents to brokers, were destined for American brothels. Forced prostitution in the USA at the time was estimated as 7 per cent of the total. Rosen, Ruth, *Lost Sisterhood: Prostitution in America, 1900–1918*, Baltimore, Maryland, 1982.
20 *Haarlems Dagblad*, 27 September 1986.
21 Interview with Kathleen Barry in *Washington Post*, quoted in *Liberator*, 1991..
22 Payoke, *Annual Report*, 1993.
23 Report of the Proceedings of the Belgian Parliament, *Parliamentary Investigation into a Structured Policy on Punishing and Eradication of Traffic in Women*, 18 March 1994.
24 L. Brussa in *Volksrant*, Amsterdam, 24 November 1994.
25 European Work Conference on Traffic in Women, 1992.
26 Rafaele, Giovanni, *La Condizione delle Immigrate Extracomunitarie*.
27 Barry, Kathleen, *Female Sexual Slavery*, New York, 1981.
28 *Telegraaf*, Amsterdam, 23 June 1979.
29 ISIS.
30 *Economisch Dagblad*, Dutch newspaper, 16 October 1981.
31 FIZ, *Gekauftes Unglück: Frauenhandel in der Schweiz*, March 1992.
32 *Hervormd Nederland*, Dutch weekly newspaper, 13 November 1993.

4 Traffic and prostitution in the Netherlands

1 Vanwesenbeeck, Ine, *Prostitutes: Well-Being and Risk*, Amsterdam, 1994.
2 For working conditions in prostitution see Ine Vanwesenbeeck et al. *Hoe (ex-) prostituées zich zelf redden, een onderzoek naar hulp-zoekgedrag van prostituées*, The Hague, 1989.
3 *Telegraaf*, Amsterdam, 14 November 1987.
4 *Dagblad van Noord-Limburg*, 16 December 1992.
5 STV documentation kit.
6 She told me and other journalists this in March 1993.
7 Annual reports of STV, *Schotten en dwarsverbanden*.
8 Stichting Tegen Vrouwenhandel, *Zicht op vrouwenhandel: een methodiek van geintegreerde begeleiding van slachtoffers van vrouwen-handel*, Utrecht, 1994.
9 For the sake of anonymity, the experiences of three raids have been merged into one.
10 Fijnaut, Cyrill, 'De Officier van Justitie en de Bende van de Miljradair', *Politiestudies*, 12, Arnhem and Antwerp, 1993.
11 Boer, Marga de, *Vrouwenhandel: beleid in beeld, eindrapport evaluatie van de PG-richtlijnen voor de opsporing en vervolging van vrouwenhandel*, Utrecht, 1994. (Soon to be published in English.)
12 Stichting Tegen Vrouwenhandel, *Barriers and Throughways, Annual Reports, 1992–94* (English translation), Utrecht, 1995.
13 Ibid.
14 Ibid.
15 This law came into force in February 1994.

5 Thailand to Europe: a one-way ticket

1 Research by Nelleke van der Vleuten, *Nieuwsbrief van de Stichting Tegen Vrouwenhandel*, year 5, 1993.
2 The Thai expert Siriporn Skrobanek distinguished these patterns of migration of women in Thailand. Documentation workshop Vienna, 1993.
3 *Volkskrant*, Amsterdam, 1 February 1994.
4 *Trouw*, Amsterdam, 31 January 1994.
5 ISIS, *Let Our Silenced Voices Be Heard, International Information Pack*, series no. 3, March 1993.
6 Ibid., and *Zaanlander*, Dutch regional newspaper, 27 February 1982.
7 ANP, Dutch press agency, 11 February 1992.
8 *Nieuwsblad van het Noorden*, Dutch regional newspaper, 30 March 1990.
9 STV, *Newsletter*, nos 3 and 4, 1991.

6 Colombian gangs: they see everything

1 Lecture by A. Peters, study day, 15 April 1989, Soeterijntheater, Amsterdam.
2 BBC, *Panorama*, 2 December 1983.
3 *Elsevier*, Dutch weekly journal, 6 November 1979.
4 *Panorama*.
5 *Telegraaf*, Amsterdam, 7 August 1985; *Volksrant*, Amsterdam, 15 September 1985; *Parool*, Amsterdam, 4 October 1985.
6 Various prostitutes and field workers.

7 Keeping it in the family

1 Part of this chapter has been published before in the Dutch weekly paper, *De Groene*.
2 *Brabants Nieuwsblad*, 25 July 1987.

8 The Greek connection

1 Yolanda Terenzio, article in *La Prostitution, quelques problèmes actuels*, Congrès de Cambridge, 27–30 September 1960, Edition van Fédération Abolitioniste Internationale, Geneva.
2 The names of victims have been changed, but the names of suspects have not been when they were reported elsewhere.
3 *Limburger*, 10 February 1994.
4 Stoop, Chris de, *Ze zijn zo lief meneer*, Leuven, 1992.
5 O'Callaghan, Sean, *Der weisse Sklavenhandel*, Berlin and Vienna, 1967.
6 Mens, Lucie van, *Prostitutie in bedrijf: organisatie, management en arbeidsverhoudingen in seksclubs in priviéhuizen*, Delft, 1992.
7 *Reformatorisch Dagblad*, Dutch newspaper, 19 December 1987.
8 Anderson, Bridget, *Britain's Secret Slaves: An Investigation into the Plight of Overseas Domestic Workers*, Kalayaan and Anti-Slavery Society.

9 The Belgian Billionaire gang

1 Stoop, Chris de, *Ze zijn zo lief meneer*, Leuven, 1992. I am also indebted to his articles in the Belgian magazine *Knack* and for information he volunteered.
2 According to the neighbour of the Billionaire.
3 Trioen, Dirk, *Boter op het hoofd*, Antwerp, 1993.

4   Mens, Lucie van, *Prostitutie in bedrijf: organisatie, management en arbeidsverhoudingen in seksclubs en privéhuizen*, Delft, 1992.
5   Slats, Jos, 'Pluk ze kaal leert het wel', in *Volkskrant*, Amsterdam, 4 January 1992.
6   Trioen, *Boter op het hoofd*.
7   *Vrije Volk*, Dutch newspaper, 21 August 1987.
8   Fijnaut, Cyrill, *Politiële corruptie in Nederland*, Arnhem, 1993.
9   Ibid.
10 *Nieuwe Revu*, Dutch weekly newspaper, 22 September 1993.
11 During the filming of 'Women Trade' for the BBC series *Inside Story*.
12 Trioen, *Boter op het hoofd*.
13 BBC, 'Women Trade'.
14 I was present at this meeting.
15 *Washington Post*, 8 September 1993.
16 Detailed in the writings of Chris de Stoop.
17 See articles by Chris de Stoop in *Knack*.

10   'I'll be safer in Yugoslavia than in the Netherlands'

1   In 1992 in Vienna 50 reports were made by women against traffickers.
2   *Telegraaf*, Amsterdam, 25 January 1993.

11   The red mafia

1   *Leeuwarder Courant*, Dutch newspaper, 7 June 1994.
2   TV2, Netherlands, 15 February 1994.
3   *Volksrant*, Amsterdam, 26 January 1993.
4   As read by the judge at the trial.
5   *Limburgs Dagblad*, 16 June 1994.
6   Asta is not her real name.
7   According to Wieslawa Stzylkowska.
8   VER magazine, *Relax*, no. 3. 1993.
9   *Algemeen Politieblad*, Dutch police magazine, 16 November 1993.
10 TV2, 15 February 1994. In Bulgaria there are also networks active in trafficking. One day a Bulgarian found by chance a trunkful of documents from 500 women, who had been forced into prostitution in surrounding countries. *Gooi Eemlander*, Dutch newspaper, 17 January 1994.
11 *Leidsch Dagblad*, Leiden, 13 November 1992.
12 *Sallands Dagblad*, Dutch regional newspaper, 6 July 1993.
13 *Nieuwe Rotterdamse Courant*, 16 January 1993.

12 Mail-order marriage

1 Rosario, Virginia O., *Lifting the Smoke Screen: Dynamics of Mail-Order Bride Migration from the Philippines*, The Hague, 1994; Delvaux, Agnes, 'Achter de sluier van het schijnhuwelijk in relatie tot vrouwenhandel in Nederland en het Caribisch gebied', unpublished, STV archives, Utrecht, July 1990.
2 *Kro Brandpunt*, Dutch TV programme, 20 February 1994.
3 Rosario, *Lifting the Smoke Screen*.
4 *Algemeen Dagblad*, Dutch newspaper, 28 October 1983.
5 VPRO (Dutch TV broadcasting organization), *Lopende Zaken*, 18 April 1993; and Pas, Sandra van de, 'De Schijn van Schijn-huwelijken', *Nieuwsbrief van de Stichting Tegen Vrouwenhandel*, STV newsletter, no. 1, 1994.
6 As read by the judge.

13 The trade in domestic workers

1 Namely the present author.
2 Kootstra, Trijntje, 'Vrouwenhandel: de invloed van de europese eenwording', University of Groningen, paper, April 1992.
3 In the Netherlands the Philippine women's group Bayanihan helps these victims.
4 According to an informant at an embassy in the Netherlands.
5 Information provided by the organization Payoke.
6 *Sunday Telegraph*, London, 13 November 1994.
7 All these instances are well documented in Anderson, Bridget, *Britain's Secret Slaves: An Investigation into the Plight of Overseas Domestic Workers*, Kalayaan and Anti-Slavery Society.
8 One-third of Philippine domestic workers report sexual abuse by their employers: Asian and Pacific Development Centre, *Trade in Domestic Helpers: Causes, Mechanisms and Consequences, Selected Papers from the Planning Meeting on International Migration and Women, Quezon City, Philippines, 30 November–5 December 1987*, Kuala Lumpur, 1989.
9 270 domestic workers, a minority of them males, reported the following (in Anderson, *Britain's Secret Slaves*):

   1 per cent psychological abuse
   4 per cent physical abuse
   3 per cent regular denial of food
   4 per cent not having a bedroom
   3 per cent not having own bed
   3 per cent imprisonment
   83 per cent confiscation of passport
   74 per cent not paid as promised.

10 In Kuwait alone 2,000 domestic helpers are sexually abused. *Drentsche Courant*, Dutch regional newspaper, 17 July 1993.
11 Anderson, *Britain's Secret Slaves*.
12 Ibid.
13 *Arab Times*, 2 November 1988.
14 *Haagsche Courant*, The Hague, 4 November 1993.
15 Anderson, *Britain's Secret Slaves*.
16 Ibid.
17 Asian and Pacific Development Centre, *Trade in Domestic Helpers*.
18 Informant from an embassy and Kaplan, David E. and Dubro, Alec, *Yakuza*, Utrecht, 1987.
19 *Gooi en Eemlander*, Dutch regional newspaper, 13 July 1989.
20 BBC, 'Body Parts Business', *Everyman*. An expert in the European Parliament, Henk Prummel, said in 1992, 'The problems of organs should be formalized, otherwise you'll settle for a huge illegal market because there is a large demand. But how to regulate it? Does the family inherit the valuable organs of the deceased? If that is the case the family will have to pay the physicians who take out the organs. You might say the organs fall under the heading of the law on the disposal of the dead. And how about gold teeth or pacemakers? Pacemakers are worth a lot of money, but they have to be removed for the safety of the crematorium.'

14 Nobody's business

1 Vleuten, N. van der, 'Survey on "Traffic in Women"', *Vena Working Paper*, Leiden, 1991.
2 Potts, Lydia, 'Weltmarkt für Arbeitskraft, von der Kolonialisation Amerikas bis zu den Migrationen der Gegenwart', dissertation, Hamburg, 1988.
3 See in the Bibliography publications of Jean D'Cunha on India, Rudie van den Berg on Puerto Rico, Kalayaan on the Philippines and Ine Vanwesenbeeck on the Netherlands. Interpol discovers 50 major rings of traffickers yearly.
4 For extensive documentation on theories of the psychological make up of prostitutes see Vanwesenbeeck, Ine, *Prostitutes: Well-Being and Risk*, Amsterdam, 1994, and Mens, Lucie van, *Prostitutie in bedrijf: organisatie, management en arbeidsverhoudingen in seksclubs in privéhuizen*, Delft, 1992.
5 Conradi, Peter, *De Rostov Ripper: het gruwelijke verhaal van Andrej Tsjikatilo, de russische seriemoordenaar*, Antwerp, 1993.
6 Hecke, Geert van, *De slavenroute*, Groot-Bijgaarden, 1994.
7 Vanwesenbeeck, *Prostitutes: Well-Being and Risk*.
8 Stichting Tegen Vrouwenhandel, *Zicht op vrouwenhandel: een methodiek van geintegreerde begeleiding van slachtoffers van vrouwenhandel*, Utrecht, 1994.

Bibliography

Abadinsky, Howard, *Organized Crime*, Boston, 1981.

AGISRA, *Frauenhandel und Prostitutionstourismus: Eine Bestandsaufnahme*, Munich, 1990.

Ammelrooy, Anneke van, *Vrouwenhandel*, The Hague, 1989.

Anderson, Bridget, *Britain's Secret Slaves: An Investigation into the Plight of Overseas Domestic Workers*, Kalayaan and Anti-Slavery Society.

Anti-Slavery International, *Forced Prostitution in Turkey*, 1993.

Asian and Pacific Development Centre, *Trade in Domestic Helpers: Causes, Mechanisms and Consequences, Selected Papers from the Planning Meeting on International Migration and Women, Quezon City, Philippines, 30 November–5 December 1987*, Kuala Lumpur, 1989.

Balkestein, J., *Dossier over de handel in vrouwen en meisjes*, 1901–2, in the archives of Meester A. de Graafstichting, Institute for Prostitution Affairs, Amsterdam.

Bardsley, Barney, *Flowers in Hell: An Investigation into Women and Crime*, London and New York, 1987.

Barlay, S., *Die Sexhändler*, Vienna and Hamburg, 1967.

Barry, Kathleen, *Female Sexual Slavery*, New York, 1981.

Barry, Kathleen, *The Prostitution of Sexuality: The Global Exploitation of Women*, New York and London, 1995.

Berg, Rudie van den, 'Las Mariposas de la Noche', Paper, Culturele Antropologie, Utrecht, December 1993.

Bernaldo de Quirós, G. and Lianas, Aguilaniedo, *Prostitution und Verbrechertum in Madrid*, Berlin, 1909.

Bianchi, Herman, *Basismodellen in de kriminologie*, Deventer, 1980.

Boer, Marga de, *Vrouwenhandel: beleid in beeld, eindrapport evaluatie van de PG-richtlijnen voor de opsporing en vervolging van vrouwenhandel*, Utrecht, 1994. (Soon to be published in English.)

Botte, Marie-France and Mari, Jean Paul, *De Prijs van een kind*, Baarn, 1994.

Bouchier, Tineke and Jong, Harry de, *Hoerenlopers, mannen op zoek naar intimiteit*, Groningen, 1987.

Bovenkerk, Frank, *Hedendaags kwaad: criminologische opstellen*, Amsterdam, 1992.

Box, Steven, *Crime and Mystification*, London, 1985.

Boyle, Sharon, *Working Girls and Their Men*, London, 1994.

Braidotti, Rosi, 'Als vrouw is de hele wereld mijn land', *Lover*, Dutch feminist magazine, no. 3, 1991.

Branssen, Els, *Vogelvrij: prostitutietoerisme en vrouwenhandel*, Utrecht, 1984.

Bristow, Edward J., *Prostitution and Prejudice: The Jewish Fight against White Slavery, 1870–1939*, New York, 1982.

Brussa, L., *Vooronderzoek naar de positie van buitenlandse prostituées in Amsterdam*, Bureau Coördinatie Vrouwenemancipatie, Amsterdam, 1987.

Bruun, Kettil, Pann, Lynn and Rexed, Ingemar, *The Gentlemen's Club: International Control of Drugs and Alcohol*, Chicago and London, 1975.

Buijs, H. and Verbraken, A., *Vrouwenhandel*, Dutch Ministry of Social Affairs, 1985.

Bullough, Vern L., *The History of Prostitution*, New York, 1964.

Calvi, Gabrizio, *De la Mafia de 1950 à nos jours*, Paris, 1986.

Carlen, Pat and Collison, Mike, *Radical Issues in Criminology*, Oxford, 1980.

Carter, Angela, *The Sadeian Woman*, London, 1979.

Cartwright, Desmond, S., Tomson, Barbara and Schwartz, Hershey, *Gang Delinquency*, Belmont, California, 1975.

Collard, W.L.A., *De handel in blanke slavinnen*, Amsterdam, 1900.

Connor, Steve and Kingman, Sharon, *The Search for the Virus: The Scientific Discovery of AIDS and the Quest for a Cure*, Harmondsworth, 1988.

Conradi, Peter, *De Rostov Ripper: het gruwelijke verhaal van Andrej Tsjikatilo, de russische seriemoordenaar*, Antwerp, 1993.

Cools, B. and Poot, R., 'Prostitutie en gemeentelijk beleid: Den Haag', unpublished paper, July 1993.

Cornish, Derek B., *The Rational Criminal: Rational-Choice Perspectives on Offending*, New York, 1986.

Daalen, Jan van, *Sans rancune: een schokkend relaas*, Amsterdam, 1991.

Davies, Miranda (ed.), *Third World, Second Sex*, vol. 2, London and New Jersey, 1987.

D'Cunha, Jean, 'Voices in the Dark', *Eve's Weekly*, May 1984.

D'Cunha, Jean, *Paper Presented at the Congress on Prostitution, Human Rights, Health and Feminism*, Brussels, 1986.

D'Cunha, Jean, 'Prostitution in a Patriarchal Society', *Economic and Political Weekly*, 7 November 1987.

D'Cunha, Jean, *The Legalization of Prostitution: A Sociological Inquiry into the Laws Relating to Prostitution in India and the West*, Bangalore, 1991.

Delvaux, Agnes, 'Achter de sluier van het schijnhuwelijk in relatie tot vrouwenhandel in Nederland en het Caribisch gebied', unpublished, STV archives, Utrecht, July 1990.

Deug, Febe, *En dan ben je pas echt ver van huis*, Utrecht, 1990.

Doelder, H. de, *Bestrijding van EEG fraude*, Gouda and Arnhem, 1990.

Dominicaanse Nieuwsbrief, year 1, no. 1.

Downes, D. and Rock, P. (eds), *Deviant Interpretations*, Oxford, 1979.

Dropkin, Israel and Viano, Emilio, *Victimology: A New Focus, Violence and Its Victims*, vols IV and V, Toronto and London, 1975.

Dutch Ministry of Justice, *Rapport van de Werkgroep Vrouwenhandel*, The Hague, 1988.

Enloe, Cynthia, *Bananas, Beaches and Bases: Making Feminist Sense of International Politics*, London, 1989.

Fédération Abolitioniste, *La Prostitution, quelques problèmes actuels*, Congrès de Cambridge, 27–30 September 1960, Edition de Fédération Abolitioniste Internationale, Geneva.

Fijnaut, Cyrill, 'De Officier van Justitie en de Bende van de Miljardair', *Politiestudies*, 12, Arnhem and Antwerp, 1993.

Fijnaut, Cyrill, *Politiële corruptie in Nederland*, Arnhem, 1993.

FIZ, *Gekauftes Unglück: Frauenhandel in der Schweiz*, March 1992.

Fortean Times, The Journal of Strange Phenomena, no. 7.

Fox, Daniel M. and Fee, Elizabeth, *AIDS: The Burdens of History*, London and Berkeley, California, 1988.

'Frauenhandel in Bangladesh, das Geschaeft mit den Organen', *Tageszeitung*, German newspaper, 12 October 1988.

Gaillard, Roger, *Sex bizz: Essai sur l'amour gris, la prostitution à Genève*, Geneva, 1981.

German Ministry for Women and Children, *Umfeld und Ausmass des Menschenhandels mit ausländische Mädchen und Frauen*, Stuttgart, 1992.

Ghana Nieuwsbrief, February 1990.

Giesen, Rose-Marie and Schumann, Gunda, *An der Front des Patriarchats*, Bensheim, 1980.

Gijsels, Hugo, *De Bende & Co: 20 Jaar Destabilisering in Belgie*, Brussels, 1990.

Graaf, Meester A. de, *De ontwikkeling van den strijd tegen de onzedelijkheid*, Utrecht, 1923.

Graaf, Ron de, 'Prostitutes and Their Clients: Sexual Networks and Determinants of Condom Use', dissertation, Amsterdam, 1995.

Graafstichting, Meester A., *Evaluatie Medisch Spreekuur Achterdam*, Amsterdam, 1982.

Gronewald, Sue, *Beautiful Merchandise: Prostitution in China, 1860–1936*, New York, 1982.

Groothuyse, J.W., *Het Menselijk Tekort van de Pooier*, Amsterdam, 1973.

Hecke, Geert van, *De slavenroute*, Groot-Bijgaarden, 1994.

Heering, Aart, 'Fenomenologie van de Steekpenning', *Intermediair*, Dutch monthly magazine, 6 November 1992.

Henriques, Fernando, *Stews and Strumpets*, part 1, London, 1961.

Heyl, Barbara, *The Madam as Entrepreneur*, New Brunswick, New Jersey, 1979.

Huitzing, A., *Betaalde liefde: prostituées in Nederland, 1850–1900*, Bergen, 1983.

Hulpverlening aan vluchtelingen en asielzoekers, publication of the Dutch Ministry of Healthcare, Welfare and Culture, Rijswijk, 1988.

ISIS, *Let Our Silenced Voices Be Heard, International Information Pack*, series no. 3, March 1993. Available from ISIS, International Women's Information and Communication Service, P.O. Box 1837, Quezon City Main, Quezon City 1100, Philippines, price US$6.

Kalayaan, *Labour Trade, Filipino Migrant Workers around the World*, London, 1987.

Kaplan, David, E. and Dubro, Alec, *Yakuza*, Utrecht, 1987.

Kerr, Austin K., *Organised for Prohibition: A New History of the Anti-Saloon League*, Yale, 1985.

Kootstra, Trijntje, 'Vrouwenhandel: de invloed van de europese eenwording', University of Groningen, paper, April 1992.

Latza, Berit, *Sextourismus in Suedostasien*, Frankfurt-am-Main, 1987.

Light, Evan, 'The Ethnic Vice Industry', *American Sociological Review*, vol. 42, 1977.

Lipka, Susanne, *Das kaufliche Glück in Sudostasien: Heirathandel und Sextourismus*, Munster, 1985.

Lombroso, C. and Ferrero, G., *Das Weib als Verbrecherin und Prostituierte*, German translation, Hamburg, 1894.

MacDonald, Eileen, *Schiet eerst de vrouwen neer*, Weert, 1992.

Mancini, J.L., *Prostitutes and Their Parasites: An Historical Survey*, London, 1963.

Masters, William H., Johnson, Virginia E. and Kolodny, Robert C., *De AIDS crisis, seks in het AIDStijdperk*, Amsterdam, 1988.

Mens, Lucie van, *Prostitutie in bedrijf: organisatie, management en arbeidsverhoudingen in seksclubs en privéhuizen*, Delft, 1992.

Mernissi, Fatima, *Achter de sluier*, Amsterdam, 1985.

Michaelson, L. (ed.) *And the Poor Get Children*, New York and London, 1981.

Middelburg, Bart, *De Mafia in Amsterdam*, Amsterdam, 1988.

Miner, Maude E., *Slavery of Prostitution: A Plea for Emancipation*, New York, 1916.

Miralao, Virginia A., Carlos, Celia O. and Fulleros Santos, Aido, *Women Entertainers in Angeles and Olongapo: A Survey Report*, Kalayaan, Quezon City, August 1990.

Mizuho, Matsuda, 'Traded Women', Japanese news article, STV archives, Utrecht.

Mouvement du Nid, *Les Jeunes et la prostitution*, October 1990.

Nawal El Saadawi, *The Hidden Face of Eve: Women in the Arab World*, London, 1980.

Newsletter, Netherlands Quarterly of Human Rights, Rights of Women, vol. 6, Edition Sim, no. 4, 1988.

O'Callaghan, Sean, *Der weisse Sklavenhandel*, Berlin and Vienna, 1967.

O'Grady, Ron, *Gebrochene Rosen: Kinderprostitution und Tourismus in Asien*, Bad Honnef, 1992.

Okyrame, bi-monthly newsletter for Ghanaians in Holland, May–June 1990.

Oste, Marielle, *Gigolos: gesprekken met escort boys en hoerenjongens*, The Hague, 1989.

Pheterson, Gail, *The Whore Stigma*, Ministry of Social Affairs, The Hague, September 1986.

Philippine Women's Support Committee, *Filipina-British Marriage Bureaux: A Report*, London, 1987.

Pileggi, Nicholas, *Wiseguy: Life in a Mafia Family*, New York, 1985.

Potts, Lydia, 'Weltmarkt für Arbeitskraft, von der Kolonialisation Amerikas bis zu den Migrationen der Gegenwart', dissertation, Hamburg, 1988.

Rafaele, Giovanni, *La Condizione delle Immigrate Extracomunitarie.*

Reitman, Ben, L., *The Second Oldest Profession*, New York, 1931.

Report of the Proceedings of the Belgian Parliament, *Parliamentary Investigation into a Structured Policy on Punishing and Eradication of Traffic in Women*, 18 March 1994.

Robertson, Frank, *The Triangle of Death: The Inside Story of the Triads, the Chinese Mafia*, London, 1977.

Roe, Clifford, *The Great War on White Slavery*, 1911.

Roerink, Alide and Vleuten, Nelleke van der, *Handel in illusies: prostitutietoerisme in Thailand*, Nijmegen, 1988.

Rosario, Virginia O., *Lifting the Smoke Screen: Dynamics of Mail-Order Bride Migration from the Philippines*, The Hague, 1994.

Rosen, Ruth, *Lost Sisterhood: Prostitution in America, 1900–1918*, Baltimore, Maryland, 1982.

Roshier, Bob, *Controlling Crime: Classical Perspective in Criminology*, Milton Keynes, 1989.

Rosier, Odette, 'Knelpunten in de bestrijding van vrouwenhandel', unpublished paper, November 1989.

Roth, Jürgen and Frey, Marc, *Het verenigd Europa van de Mafia*, Amsterdam and Leuven, 1994.

Schalken, T.M., 'Anonieme getuige en strafvorderlijke logistiek', *Nederlands Juristenblad*, January 1990.

Schmidt, Heinz G., *Kindermarkt: Reportagen von schmutzigsten Geschaft der Welt*, Basle, 1988.

Schulte, Regina, *Sperrbezirke: Tugendhaftigkeit und Prostitution in der bürgerlichten Welt*, Frankfurt-am-Main, 1979.

Segeth, Uwe Volker, *Kinder die sich Verkaufen*, Frankfurt-am-Main and Vienna, 1980.

Sellmann, A. *50 Jahre Kampf für Volkssittlichkeit und Volkskraft*, Schwelm, Westfalen, 1935.

Shizuko, Ohshima and Francis, Carolyn, *Japan through the Eyes of Woman Migrant Workers*, edition of HELP, Asian Women's Shelter, Tokyo, 1989.

Slats, Jos, 'Pluk ze kaal leert het wel', *Volkskrant*, Amsterdam, 4 January 1992.

Smart, Carol, *Women, Crime and Criminology*, London, 1967.

Smart, Carol (ed.), *Women, Sexuality and Social Control*, London, 1978.

Sörensen, Patsy, *De maskers af, over socialisme, prostitutie en mensenhandel*, Berne and Antwerp, 1994.

Stemvers, F.A., *Meisjes van plezier: de geschiedenis van de prostitutie in Nederland*, Weesp, 1985.

Stichting Imperialisme en Onderzoek, *Latijnsamerikaanse vakbeweging en solidariteit: kritische analyse van clat in Latijnsamerika en Nederland*, Nijmegen, 1984.

Stichting Tegen Vrouwenhandel, *Verslag van de europese conferentie vrouwenhandel*, The Hague, 1991.

Stichting Tegen Vrouwenhandel, *Barriers and Throughways, Annual Reports, 1992–4* (English translation).

Stichting Tegen Vrouwenhandel, *Zicht op vrouwenhandel: een methodiek van geïntegreerde begeleiding van slachtoffers van vrouwenhandel*, Utrecht, 1994.

Stoop, Chris de, *Ze zijn zo lief meneer*, Leuven, 1992.

Thai Development, vol. 4, no. 1, 1986.

Trioen, Dirk, *Boter op het hoofd*, Antwerp, 1993.

Truong, T., *Sex, Money and Morality: The Political Economy of Prostitution and Tourism in South-East Asia*, Amsterdam, 1988.

Tübinger Projektgruppe, *Frauenhandel in Deutschland*, Bonn, 1989.

United Nations Economic and Social Commission for Asia and the Pacific (ESCAP), *Report of the Workshop of Experts on Prevention and Rehabilitation Schemes for Young Women in Prostitution and Related Occupations*, Bangkok, 11–17 June 1985.

Van der Roer, Robert, 'De miljoenengok van Ger van D.V.', in Cyrill Fijnaut (ed.), *Georganiseerde misdaad en politiebeleid*, Lochem, 1989.

Vanwesenbeeck, Ine, 'Sekswerk als professionele zorgarbeid: de straat en de club', *Lover*, Dutch feminist magazine, no. 1, 1991.

Vanwesenbeeck, Ine, *Prostitutes: Well-Being and Risk*, Amsterdam, 1994.

Vanwesenbeeck, I., Groen M. and Altink Sietske, *Hoe (ex-) prostituées zich zelf redden: een onderzoek naar hulpzoekgedrag van prostituées, een uitgave het Ministerie van Sociale Zaken*, The Hague, 1989.

Vena Newsletter, 'Traffic in Women', November 1989.

Visser, Jan, *Beroep prostituée*, Utrecht, 1987.

Vleuten, N. van der, 'Survey on "Traffic in Women"', *Vena Working Paper*, Leiden, 1991.

Vulto, Marij, *Een Kwestie van Overleven*, report by Meester de Graafstichting, Amsterdam, 1983.

Wagenaar, Agnes and Velde, Feikje van der, 'Vrouwenhandel, een Moderne vorm van slavernij', paper, Amsterdam, March 1990.

Walkowitz, Judith R., *City of Dreadful Delight*, Chicago, 1992.

Winick, Charles and Kinsie, Paul M., *The Lively Commerce*, Chicago, 1971.

Wong Lun Hing, F.J.H., *Prostitutie*, Utrecht, 1961.